D1487334

Body
language
Secrets

Body language *Secrets*

A Guide During Courtship And Dating

Book and Photography by *DYNAMITE*
Cover by A&M, Box 2926, Kona HI 96745
Models: Joanna Bardot Lopez, Andrea Rodriguez
Tom Horsley, R. Don Steele

Cataloging in Publication Data
Main entry under title:

Steele, R. Don
    Body Language Secrets: A Guide During Courtship And Dating

    p. cm.
Includes index

ISBN 0-9620671-6-4

1. Courtship and dating
2. Nonverbal communication
3. Relationships

Manufactured in the United States of America

First Printing: June 1997, this printing September 2002

10 9 8 7 6

To

Joanna

Your love transformed me.

PREFACE

Manuscript reviewers who were politically correct, gender-neutralists, protested that the book is written *as though it is natural, as well as necessary*, for the male to be the initial aggressor during courtship.

Not Guilty! I simply take for granted that most of the time men must get things started. Should this offend you, please be assured that no offense is intended. My approach to *explaining* courtship does not mean that assertive, 90s women must stand and wait.

Several female reviewers complained that it was slanted toward helping men. *Nolo Contendre!* I'm a man, often explaining things from a man's viewpoint. No favoritism is intended.

Some English majors objected to awkward wording such as . . . *he, or she, is lying* . . . as well the grammatically incorrect but politically correct use of *they* or *their* when the subject is singular as in *Everyone wants to have their [his] cake and eat it too.*

Guilty! A person cannot please all other human beings and I tried anyway. Please try to overlook such shortcomings.

A few 50ish reviewers accused me of being an *ageist*. I assured them, as I assure you, that although I use younger people in many of the explanations and examples of courtship rituals, everything applies to people of all ages.

Finally, several reviewers, fans from previous books, protested that the overall tone is too serious. They are familiar with my style of using personal success and failure stories to enlighten while entertaining. If my final result is still to serious, I am sorry. I did what I thought was effective.

My firm conviction that people everywhere are fundamentally the same is behind everything I have written. Archeological and anthropological evidence that we, the people who live at the dawn of the 21st Century, are essentially the same as the people who lived 15,000 years ago at the dawn of civilization is the foundation of this book. However, most of that factual information is reserved for the Appendix.

Our culture, Western Civilization, has come up with hundreds of things, literally, that men and women must do during courtship, when these things must be done, and how they must be done. However, we must understand that over the last 60 million years, during the rise of mammals, the natural world created us all, evolved us all and armed us all with behaviors, drives and hungers for a single purpose—survival. Why? So that each of us lives long enough to send our DNA into the future. That's what courtship is *really* all about.

That fact underlies much of what I have written. Once again, no offense intended. As with everything you read, keep the parts that you can use to improve your life, and discard the rest.

One feminist strongly objected to the entire manuscript. "Women should simply walk right up to men they find attractive." I asked if she read what *female* anthropologists had to say on that topic. Her reply, "I don't agree with them, either!" What can I say? A person cannot please every human being.

One last thing. A few reviewers were put off by my casual writing style and refusal to use 50-cent words. Their comment, "Sure, it's easy to read and understand, but it's not 'professional', people won't take it seriously." I cited Robert Heinlein's advice to writers, "Eschew obfuscation." A couple of them got it. For those who didn't, I offered a slightly modified version of George Bernard Shaw's well-known, "He who can, does. He who cannot, teaches." [And writes books about how to do it]. That had the desired effect.

Enjoy!

CONTENTS

ACKNOWLEDGMENTS

A simple, but deeply felt thank you to Nathaniel Branden. You saved my life in 1972. By 1975, with your guidance and insistence, I had learned the fundamentals of how to live, truly live, that life you saved. Without you, none of this, or any of my fully, alive, joyous journey of discovery through life, would have been possible.

As always, to my daughter, Syndee, thanks for just being you! By doing so, my journey has substance and meaning.

To Joanna, my wife, thanks for enduring what a writer must do as this book slowly came together across time, distance, heartbreak and happiness.

Thanks to all the acquaintances, colleagues and friends who gave me what a writer needs most, negative, constructive feedback. As you remember, after five years, I could not see the forest for the trees.

And finally, to the nameless Disco Dick at Bobby McGee's, Fullerton, California in the summer of 1982, thank you for erasing my final sliver of doubt about the validity of body language.

ABOUT THE AUTHOR

Don's first job was in 1952, age 12. In the heart of Appalachia, he was the Saturday telephone operator in his hometown of Shippenville, Pennsylvania, population 258. He earned ten cents an hour. At 16 he worked as an embalmer's assistant for the summer. The next summer he was an oiler of strip mining equipment, a muddy, cold, dreary, dangerous task. Those two jobs convinced him to get an education.

He attended Clarion State, Penn State, USC and Cal State Fullerton for a BA in Philosophy and Cal State Northridge for his MA in Psychology. He interned with Nathaniel Branden in Beverly Hills. After becoming a Marriage, Family and Child Counselor in 1976, he worked with Branden and was in private practice until 1990. He began writing professionally in 1984. Additionally, Don worked for more than 20 aerospace, defense and engineering companies as well as the Republican National Committee and many political campaigns.

He conducts workshops and seminars on Body Language, Office Politics, Dressing for Success as well as Dating-Social Skills in Los Angeles. In February 2002, Don began hosting a LIVE CALL IN RADIO SHOW. Listen at his website http://steelballs.com.

Beyond writing, other passions include a deep, abiding hatred for bureaucrats, poverty pimps and nearly all politicians; a lifelong devotion to anthropology, philosophy; astronomy and cosmology.

He and Joanna live in Whittier, California with their dogs Wolfie and Tootsie, cats Princess, Snookums and Puppy and rabbit Peaches.

We must, however, acknowledge,
as it seems to me, that man,
with all his noble qualities, with sympathy
which feels for the most debased,
with benevolence which extends not only to
other men but to the humblest living
creatures, with his God-like intellect
which has penetrated into the movements and
constitution of the solar system,
with all these exalted powers,
man still bears within his bodily frame the
indelible stamp of his lowly origins.

CHARLES DARWIN

Better to have loved and lost
than to have never loved at all.

(LORD) ALFRED TENNYSON

What's It All About?

Nearly every book on dating and relating, as well as many books on body language, are written by experts as opposed to *doers*. What's a doer? Someone who does what he, or she, is helping you learn.

THIS BOOK IS REALISTIC

Unlike most self-help books, this is a *how-to* book, *when-to* book, *what-to* book and *who-to* book by a man who has used, and taught, courtship body language for the past 25 years, and continues to!

You are going to learn FACTS. Tomorrow morning, you will put those facts to work for you.

VERBAL INTERCOURSE FUNDAMENTALS

Here are crucial statistics about how we homo sapiens communicate with each other during courtship. Everything you are about to learn is based on these facts.

- People form 90 percent of their opinion about you in the first 90 seconds.

- Communication is 60 percent nonverbal and 40 percent verbal. Of the verbal portion, *only* 10 percent is accomplished by the words themselves! The other 30 percent is done by how the words are spoken, inflection and tone of voice.

- Nonverbal communication is achieved by eye contact, posture, gestures, position relative to the listener and the attire of the speaker. But that is *not* the most significant fact. Here it is—*nonverbal signals have* five *times more impact than verbal signals.*

THE SITUATION

You want to become far more effective at finding, meeting, talking with, and dating the right kind of person.

Find. This is not meant to be glib, but I explain in only a few pages where to look for the right kind of person. Hint! Not in bars, clubs or any other pickup spots. More later.

Meet. I don't want to give the impression that it's child's play to meet someone. But, *Meeting Mr Or Ms Right* is only about five percent of the book. I'm certain you will put a few of the techniques from that chapter to work for you this weekend!

I'm supremely confident that in the immediate future, you'll get much better at meeting people you're interested in. Why am I so confident? Because you will have found them in the right places!

Talk With. Can you carry on a simple conversation and pay attention to the other person's gestures? That's all there is to it, once you know what to look for.

At first, you won't notice all of the signals coming at you. But soon, most of what he, or she, is saying *without* words will become stunningly obvious. After you get that down, you'll be sending the other person unspoken messages you want them to *hear!*

Date the right kind of person. This is the essence of the book. All of the body language and most of the concrete, practical methods and strategies come together to make it possible for you to identify, then attract *the right kind of person.*

IS BODY LANGUAGE FOR REAL?

In the late 1800s, Charles Darwin noted that the meaning of many human gestures was the same the world over. He also noted that some human gestures had the same meaning for the apes as they did for us!

About 70 years later, the science of kinesics, the technical name for body language, was formalized by Dr. Ray Birdwhistell in the early 1950s. However, I learned the most about this fascinating subject by working with psychotherapist Nathaniel Branden, PhD and from books by Albert E. Scheflen and Gerald I. Nierenberg. Yes, it's for real. As you will see shortly.

HELPFUL HINT

If you didn't take time to read the *Preface*, take a moment before you continue. It sets the stage so you can learn more, then easily remember it.

THE GENDER GAP

During courtship and dating, women do not face the same types of problems as men. How's that for an understatement!

A man usually says he's not able to tell if a woman is really interested in him. Whereas, the most common problem a woman faces is not being able to quickly determine if he's a lurking Mr. Hyde or a potential Mr. Right.

Let's attack the woman's problem first. The next chapter is called *Lines, Lies Or The Truth.*

Men, as you read the chapter, put yourself in the woman's shoes. That's the quickest way to become more effective at social intercourse.

You knew I was a snake
when you let me in.

THE SNAKE TO THE RABBIT AS HE BEGAN TO EAT HIM.
The snake was dying from the cold outside in the storm. He sincerely promised not to act like a snake if he could just get warm by the fire. AESOP'S FABLE.

Lines, Lies Or The Truth

Courtship *feels* dangerous. Everyone fears being rejected or humiliated and hurt. So, a genuine person is slightly nervous when meeting someone who rings his, or her, chimes. Sincere people are always somewhat awkward and childish no matter how hard they try to be cool and relaxed. Even if forty-something, they may blush or stutter because this is real, this is important, this is arousing, and this could get your heart broken.

But the experienced manipulator or game player is not afraid because he, or she, knows it is just that, a game. He can't get hurt, because he's not going to be genuinely vulnerable.

A SINCERE MAN

How can you tell if he's sincere? Look at his body language. Is what he's saying with words in sync with what he's saying without words? If anything is inconsistent, be on the alert. Probe deeper with subtle questions as you quietly concentrate on his gestures and the ever reliable "vibrations."

These next few paragraphs are titled as if the information only applies to men, but *women who lie* do exactly the same things.

SIGNS OF SINCERITY

When he's standing, his feet are slightly apart, firmly planted on the ground. He looks you in the eyes often. When he gestures, his palms are open and up. His arms are slightly extended. His head is slightly tilted. He only glances at your breasts occasionally. He never sneaks a peek at other women. He leans toward you now and then to invade your territory.

Only after you have touched him, does he touch you, and then it's completely appropriate. He does not try to dominate you by getting so close that his physical size is intimidating. When sitting down, his openness and gestures are about the same as when he's standing.

A DECEITFUL MAN

When he's talking or listening, his feet are not firmly planted. One foot rests on the outside edge. Sometimes only his heel touches the floor. If he clears his throat, fidgets in the chair, touches his nose lightly, touches his lip, tugs his ear or rubs his eye, he's probably lying to you.

TOUCHES YOU BEFORE YOU TOUCH HIM

Men who are well-practiced liars know that many women are starved for touch. So, they try to manipulate you filling that need. By touching you first, he reveals himself as someone who is only interested in physical closeness.

Women who touch men almost immediately after meeting them are suspected *Rapo*, as in Rape-o, players, explained shortly.

OPENNESS IS SINCERITY *The wine glass is not a barrier, he's leaning forward, head slightly tilted, hands not clenching, feet flat on floor, eyes looking directly at you, and overall, he's alert and energetic.*

LYING EYES

Even men who are not practiced in the art of courtship deception, can force themselves to look sincere when they are deliberately lying. At least they can keep their face looking sincere.

Women, beware! Many men can look you right in the eyes and lie. It is a skill they learn when playing team sports as a child and adolescent. Later, they perfect this ability at the poker table and in the business world.

Men, pay attention! Most women have to avert their eyes when they lie to you. When they tell the truth, they can, and do, look you right in the eyes.

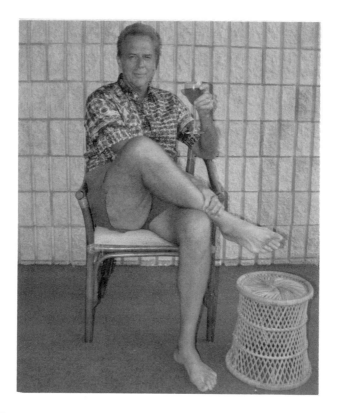

HOLDING ONTO HIMSELF OR OBJECTS *Getting a grip on his feelings, literally. Also serves to distract him from feeling the negative emotions, which are, in the case of a liar, guilt and fear of being discovered as a fraud.*

The seated liar will often cross one leg so that the ankle of the crossed leg is resting on his knee. This is a disguised method of being closed so that he feels less vulnerable. To get a grip on himself, he holds onto the shin, knee, or ankle of the crossed leg.

The grip is easily seen when the liar squeezes his drink or the arm of the chair so hard that his finger tips turn white. Notice the finger tips in the photo.

EYES CLOSE AS HE SPEAKS

This is the same as touching one's eye or rubbing one's eyes. The liar doesn't have to look you in the eyes as he lies or just after. This gesture can also reveal disdain, contempt and pomposity. It is commonly seen in people who consider themselves better then the rest of us.

MOUTH, LIP OR NOSE TOUCHING

He barely touches his chin, lip or corner of the mouth as he speaks, or just after. With this gesture the liar declares, "I can't believe I said that," or, "I can't believe what I'm saying." When he touches his nose, the liar is saying, "This stinks, even to me." The act also conveniently covers his mouth.

PALMS NOT UP WHEN GESTURING

The person appears to be carrying on an animated conversation, however he is always hiding his palms. It's a form of holding back and hiding one's true feelings.

The gesture indicates a general unwillingness to be vulnerable. It is a mild version of crossed arms or crossed legs. Remember, openness is sincerity because the speaker, or listener, has nothing to hide.

LYING FEET

Most of us can control what shows on our face because we have mastered that ability through experience and practice. However, even skilled liars and sexual users do not realize that their hands or feet can reveal them as the snakes they are. That's if you are looking for it. Pay attention!

The liar can tell his tale, or spin her web, and feel far less guilt if he does not have his feet firmly planted on the ground. Doubt the words of anyone whose feet are not flat on the floor and steady.

Caution! As children, females in our culture are taught that it is not proper to wiggle and run around like little boys do to get rid of excess energy.

Girls are admonished to "sit still like a little-lady," so they move their feet and hands. As adults, some eager, excited women fidget and squirm their feet as they hold everything above their knees in a proper, polite posture.

LYING HANDS

Patting oneself usually means the person is trying to reassure himself. It's the same as patting a child gently to let him know everything's going to be okay. It may mean that the person is taking a big risk by talking with this attractive woman so he tells himself, "everything will be fine." Then again, it could mean that he's telling himself that it's okay to lie just this one time.

Worry and anxiety are behind wringing one's hands. But a similar gesture, rubbing one's hands together means excitement and anticipation. The verbal expression that would accompany rubbing one's hands together is "Oh boy, oh boy!"

When someone pinches himself on the hand, it is often an attempt to distract himself from a powerful emotion. It could be guilt about telling a lie. It could be he's trying to hide how excited he is, or how nervous and afraid he is.

Picking at one's cuticles or nails is sometimes the same as hand pinching, but generally it means the person is angry or frustrated.

When hands are folded with fingers intertwined, it commonly means the person is trying to disguise what his hands want to divulge.

The liar often moves his hands toward his mouth or eyes during or immediately after the lie. Sometimes he rests his elbows on the table and raises his folded hands in front of his mouth and speaks from behind this barrier.

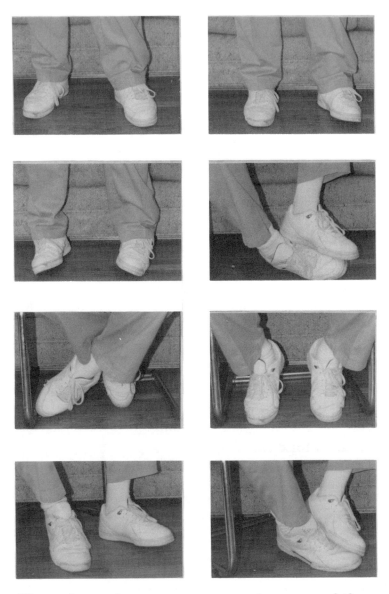

*These photos show many ways people unground them-
selves. It's an attempt at not feeling something, usually
guilt for lying but can hiding be sexual excitement.*

These gestures can also mean he doesn't believe that you really are as you present yourself. As always, it takes more data to make a firm decision.

The key to spotting a liar is to ignore all signals except his hands and feet. That includes ignoring the honeyed words we all enjoy hearing.

BEARD OR DISGUISE

A few men actually look better with a beard. For example, those with receding chins or pock-marked complexions. Occasionally a man is compensating for a bald head. Many times his beard is an attempt to make the world believe he's an intelligent authority figure. Other times, his beard is a facade that he hides behind while he manipulates you with words.

Be suspicious. Start with the attitude that he must prove himself doubly. As always, rely on your intuition.

EYEGLASSES OR MASKS

Many people wear glasses for the same reason as some men wear beards—they want others to see them as intelligent or they are hiding behind a wall of glass. The most suspicious glasses are tinted. Hiding one's eyes is always suspect. It is similar to rubbing one's eye or averting one's eyes.

MISTAKEN SIGNS OF DISHONESTY

Unless he touches his face, some postures or gestures are commonly mistaken for lying. But, they usually mean he's controlling himself, trying prevent his excitement or nervousness from showing.

When standing or sitting, if his legs are crossed, but not tightly, that's okay. When seated, if he has both hands folded, holding his knee cap, that's probably just nervousness. If he's holding his shin or calf with one or both hands, he's not open but probably isn't lying.

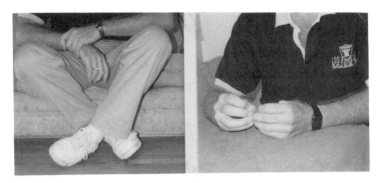

UPPER LEFT *The person is holding onto himself as well as ungrounding his feet. Either he's telling a big lie, or the emotions he's avoiding are quite powerful.*

UPPER RIGHT *The person is distracting himself by pinching and picking at his cuticles. He could be a liar or he's trying not to show his feelings.*

LOWER LEFT *Although a hand touching the face is usually disbelief or lying, this gesture means the listener is bored or he's evaluating what he's hearing.*

LOWER RIGHT *Tugging his ear means "I don't 'hear' what's being said." If listening, he does not believe what he's hearing. If talking, doesn't believe himself.*

MAJOR CLUSTER OF GESTURES *If she's talking, this woman is telling a colossal lie. If listening, she is utterly disgusted with the person who is talking.*

From top to bottom, notice all the different signals she is sending. Her head is vertical, not tilted, revealing that she is not interested. Her eyes are closed, indicating she's either telling a lie or does not believe what she's hearing.

Her finger is touching her nose as the rest of her hand covers her mouth. This indicates "something stinks," or "I don't believe what I said," or "I don't believe what I heard." She is hunched over, not sitting up erect and alert. She has closed herself off completely by crossing her arms and crossing her legs. Only one foot is on the floor and it is not solidly planted, but rocked back on the heel.

WALL OF HANDS *Talking from behind a wall of hands indicates lying or being extremely cautious with his choice of words. During courtship, this gesture means he's not open, thus probably not sincere.*

EYE RUB OR TOUCH *This gesture usually means the person can't "see" what's being said. If listening, he does not believe the speaker. If talking, he does not believe himself. Can also mean the person is bored or sleepy.*

DISGUISED EYE RUB *Even though she only touched her forehead above her eye as if to fix her hair, this gesture indicates disbelief. Notice that it is combined with a back-of-hand gesture to display a wedding ring, indicating that she is not even slightly interested.*

HAND TO MOUTH *This gesture often begins as a slight bottom-of-the-nose rub. The hand stays and covers the mouth. That means he does not believe the speaker or he's preventing himself from saying something.*

CLOSING SIGNALS

Women, do not mistake arrogance or snobbishness for confidence. Even more dangerous, beware of any man who treats you with disdain or contempt. That is not confidence. These guys dislike women and enjoy hurting them, sometimes even physically. Pay attention to your intuition. See photos of arrogance vs confidence in the upcoming chapter, *Courtship Tactics For Men.*

Men, it is usually not a good idea to chase any female for more than a few feet, figuratively, because she may enjoy running away instead of being caught, a summary version of *Rapo.* (To be explained shortly.) However, she may be playing *Catch Me And I'm Yours.* If that's the case, you must chase at least twice to pass this test of your sincerity. Much more about tests versus games is coming up in *Resistance, Reluctance And Tests.*

IT'S NOT ALL NONVERBAL

Sometimes the first clue that he's lying is his use of *exaggerated* nonverbal gestures of sincerity or confidence. Confirm your suspicion. Be on the alert for gratuitous verbal reassurances liars often use. *I wouldn't lie to you* and *Let me be truthful with you* will tip you off. Others: *I'm serious,* or *You can believe me,* plus any other rendition that causes a bystander to say, "Methinks the [snake] doth protest too much."

GAME PLAYERS AND MANIPULATORS

Eric Berne, founder of Transactional Analysis, explained these kinds of people best in his book *The Games People Play.*

Some women play *Rapo,* as in Rape-o. During the conversation she's relaxed but suggestive and appears to be eager to "jump in the sack." When the man proposes they take steps toward that end, she recoils in horror and protests loudly with some version of, "What kind of girl do you think I am?"

To win the biggest prize, she needs an audience. Her payoff? The *Rapo* player shows everyone within earshot that she is a good girl who is erotically appealing. At the same time, she proves to herself that she's attractive and desirable without the danger of emotional and sexual involvement.

Homosexual and impotent men play a similar game called *Cavalier*. The player's not going to get rejected, hurt or exposed because he's not going to follow through on his charming and gallant act.

The *Cavalier* leads her on, then when she suggests they take the first step toward a sexual union, he recoils in horror and says something like, "I'm not that sort of unrefined fellow."

Just like the *Rapo* player, the *Cavalier* needs an audience. If he's a homosexual, he wants men to notice him. If impotent, he wants everyone to think he can perform and that he's attractive sexually.

HANNIBAL AND OTHER CANNIBALS

In *Silence Of The Lambs*, Anthony Hopkins convinced us all that he *was* Hannibal The Cannibal. Skilled actors and experienced liars, such as salespeople and politicians, can control themselves so that the vast part of their of their body language is in accord with their words.

Rapo and *Cavalier* players, as well as every other type of manipulator-user of either sex, want sexual gratification without emotional involvement. Their trademarks—appearing supremely confident, poised and relaxed. That's instead of somewhat excited and nervous as genuine people are.

Another tip-off is that game players often dress for the part they are playing GQ man or sexpot. Just remember, smooth talkers are practiced experts. As always, if it's too good to be true, it ain't.

SMART WOMEN–FOOLISH CHOICES

Although women are powerfully intuitive, they often do not notice the man is lying and therefore, cannot be trusted. There are well-known reasons why some women choose deranged men.

Some women subconsciously want to be mistreated because they believe they don't deserve to be treated properly. Others are so terribly lonely they tolerate horrible behavior so they don't have to be alone. And, still other women, had neurotic fathers who didn't, and couldn't, love them. The men these women seek out are just as screwed up as their fathers. It is a futile attempt to get the love they never got from their fathers.

I think it's a combination of all this and much more that will be covered shortly. Preview—some women want *bad* boys to prove their love by changing into *good* men.

Attention Women! *WHY* someone chooses a man who will hurt her sells psychobabble, pop psychology books and fuels inane daytime TV talk shows. But, and this is a big BUT, you, alone, are responsible for making certain the man you are dating is someone who will not treat you badly.

One more time. Above all else, trust your intuition. If it feels bad, it *is* bad.

Body Language Anecdote–Becoming A True Believer

A few days after watching a video of *The Thomas Crown Affair*, Joanna and I were gazing into each other's eyes as we sipped wine and nibbled *hors d'oeuvres* in a quiet restaurant three months into our relationship. All of a sudden, she forever lost her doubts about the validity of body language.

Between intense moments of falling deeply into love, I had shared my knowledge of nonverbal communication with her as idle conversation. She was a skeptic, as most people are in the beginning. I had rented the movie as a subtle attempt at convincing her. A few hours after watching it, I rewound to the chess match and seduction scene and asked Joanna to focus on body language.

As the attractive female investigator matched wits with Thomas Crown on the chess board, and about the robbery, she used sexual signals to distract him. Every time it was his turn to move, she idly, but sensually, fondled her bishop. In blunt terms, she masturbated it. Crown could not take his eyes off what she was doing, lost concentration and gave up on chess. Joanna wasn't impressed.

Back to wine and *hors d'oeuvres.* As we were chatting, Joanna abruptly, and loudly, blurted out, "Look what I'm doing to my glass!" A few nearby diners and I looked. She was slowly and lovingly stroking the long stem, up and down, up and down.

Women, as you talk, don't hesitate to use this subtle, powerful nonverbal signal to tell the man he's doing just fine. Men, the equivalent is to run your finger slowly around the rim of your glass. If you want to be slightly blatant, casually touch the tip of your finger to your mouth now and then to lubricate the lip of the glass.

A SUGGESTION FOR WOMEN

As explained in the *Preface,* I am a man, thus, at times, I write from a man's viewpoint. Some women readers may feel that I am favoring men because of this. No, I am acting on the assumptions stated in the *Preface.*

So, women, please follow along as I advise the men. They are learning how to deal with what you women do, almost instinctively. Thus, you might be able to identify some areas that you, personally, can change so that the entire courtship effort is simplified. If so, the both of you can more easily decide if you should continue, or go on your separate ways.

SUMMING IT UP

There are sexual manipulator-users and there are game players. There are sincere people who are afraid and nervous because they have been hurt before. There are people who don't do exactly the right things because they are inexperienced or recently back in the single world. There are genuine, good people. Your job is to know who's who.

Here's a summary of the gestures liars use:

SPEAK NO EVIL	TOUCHES MOUTH
SEE NO EVIL	TOUCHES EYE
HEAR NO EVIL	TOUCHES EAR
FEEL NO EVIL	UNGROUNDED FEET

The next chapter, *What Is Body Language?* explains why we must all realize that *you cannot not communicate.*

You cannot not communicate.

UNKNOWN WISE PERSON

What Is Body Language?

For those who have difficulty believing in body language, here's one way to look at it.

You are on vacation in Moscow. Upon returning to your room, a wild-eyed, pistol wielding man confronts you. He slams the door and snarls something in Russian. As he cocks the gun and points it at your head, would you reach for your English-Russian dictionary?

To a gun toting mugger who speaks English, most of us would use body language *and* words to neutralize the threat. Body language? Yes! Raise your hands. Look as powerless and non-threatening as possible, In a pleading, helpless voice say, "Take my money. Please don't shoot. I have two kids at home."

A LANGUAGE WE ALL SPEAK

The natural experts on body language are pets and kids. My cat knows when I'm angry with her, when I'm indifferent and when I'm ready to feed her. A child knows when Mommy's happy and when Daddy's lying.

Cats have never read a body language book, and neither have kids, yet they know exactly what we (you, me, everyone) are feeling. As we are "educated" by our culture we lose our innate ability to read and speak body language.

Everything is body language—tone of voice, clearing our throats, rubbing our eyes, crossing our arms, tapping our toes, touching our nose—everything except the words we say.

Your eye contact, or lack of eye contact, communicates. Your pauses communicate. Your crossed legs communicate. Your open hands communicate. Your aroma communicates.

In particular, your appearance communicates: hair style, type of eye glasses, accessories, tattoos and your overall choice of attire.

How you are dressed is a major part of the message you *send,* but, it is an even larger part of how your listeners *receive* it. The way you are dressed dictates how others respond to you.

> *Clothes are a tool you use to control*
> *how others react to you and how they treat you.*
> JOHN MOLLOY, *DRESS FOR SUCCESS*

You cannot not communicate. No matter what you do, or don't do, you broadcast your emotional state. Even if you put on a poker face and sit perfectly still, you loudly announce, "I'm trying to hide what I'm feeling."

Each of us reveals our emotional state with nonverbal signals. During courtship, and later in a romantic relationship, knowing what the other person is feeling helps you behave appropriately. But, to know what that person is experiencing, you must attack the environment with your eyes, ears and, yes, your intuition.

WOMEN ARE BETTER THAN MEN

Women's renown intuition arises from the way biology and evolution "wired" female brains. The connection between the left half and the right half of the female brain is much larger in women than men.

Thus, women can process and integrate rational information from the left half of their brains with sensory and emotional information from the right half and know something accurately without concrete evidence. That's intuition.

> *A woman's guess is much more accurate*
> *than a man's certainty.*
> RUDYARD KIPLING

The larger connection also is the source of their ability to discern extremely subtle changes in patterns. The difference in ability between the sexes is scientifically verifiable from the age of two! NOTE 1

Attention women! During courtship and dating, use your intuition. Validate and vindicate your intuition by using what you learn from this book.

SOCIAL INTERCOURSE FUNDAMENTALS

Although a few of these were part of the introduction, take some time to think about the implications of these facts. In other words, based on this data, *what will you do during the next few courtship conversations that you have never done before?* Take your time. This information can, and will, change your social life, forever!

- People form 90 percent of their opinion about you in the first 90 seconds.

- Communication is 60 percent nonverbal and 40 percent verbal. Of the verbal portion, *only* 10 percent is accomplished by the words themselves! The other 30 percent is done by how the words are spoken, inflection and tone of voice.

- The nonverbal portion of communication is accomplished by eye contact, posture, gestures, position relative to the listener and the attire of the speaker. But that is *not* the most significant fact. Here it is—*nonverbal signals have five times the impact of verbal signals.*

• Information that is retained was received by the brain as follows: 85 percent by the eyes, 10 percent by the ears and 5 percent by touch, taste and smell.

• When the verbal and the nonverbal parts of the message are congruent, the listener believes the message. If they are incongruent, usually the speaker's words are saying *yes*, but his body is saying *no.*

One thing to do is always *dress* for success as explained two pages ago. How you are dressed gets everything started off on the right, or wrong foot. Yes, I believe that repetition is the key to learning.

Body Language Anecdote–Televised Liars As the Watergate hearings were taking place in 1973, I was completing my 3000 hour internship as a Marriage, Family and Child Counselor with Nathaniel Branden. Part of my responsibilities included learning, then teaching body language to fellow interns.

Some afternoons we'd watch the televised testimony with sorrow and dread as our country's President was slowly, but steadily revealed as a crook. I kept telling everyone John Mitchell, the Attorney General, was lying on the witness stand. But nobody believed, rather, wanted to believe, that America's chief law enforcement officer would lie to the United States Senate. No matter, I could feel it, as corny as it sounds, deep in my bones.

One day, someone turned the volume down on the television to answer the phone. We kept watching the silent screen. With the sound off, we were all able to notice that time after time, Mitchell would touch his mouth or eye when responding, or close his eyes while, or just as he finished, speaking. After he did that about three times, the entire group, especially me, screamed, "He's lying! He's lying!"

Nixon avoided impeachment by resigning, but Mitchell and many others went to prison.

Practice what you're learning. Spot liars on television. But, it's not as easy nowadays, because jury consultants who work for the defense as well as the prosecution, coach, teach and rehearse witnesses to keep their hands away from their face while on the stand. However, if the witness can be put under enough pressure, he will lose control and touch himself somewhere above the neck when he's lying.

On newscasts, see if you can catch liars. The easiest to nail are people who are not usually spokespersons, thus they have not been trained how to *appear* sincere and truthful. These include newly elected politicians, recently appointed bureaucrats, street cops and grandstanding eye witnesses Turn off the sound and refine your skills. Practice makes perfect. Practice!

As *Signs Of Interest,* the next chapter, are sent and received during the early stages of courtship, then later when dating, heed this timeless wisdom and advice no matter how trite it may sound:

Actions *speak louder than words.*
Believe what people do, *not what they say.*

NOTE 1
Many "radical" thinkers (I am one of them) believe that the physical and chemical differences between male and female brains, as well as body differences, explain most, if not all, gender-specific talents and capabilities. We also believe that these differences explain why women view courtship and relationships from an entirely different universe than men. See *BRAIN WIRING* in the Appendix.

Believe only half of what you see and none of what you hear.

UNKNOWN WISE PERSON

Signs Of Interest

Women, keep that geek away! Get that guy in the red shirt to come over here and talk. Send each man an unspoken but unmistakable message.

Men, don't get shot down because you approached a woman who is not interested in you. Pay attention to what she's *saying* without words.

Here are signs of interest sent from across the room. Most are applicable to both sexes, although a few apply only to women. Those are indicated by italics. The sequence of the list approximates the courtship sequence.

I'M INTERESTED	DON'T BOTHER ME
Sidelong glance(s)	Never sneaks a peek
Looks at you a few times	Fleeting eye contact
Holds your gaze briefly	Looks away quickly
Downcast eyes, then away	*Looks away, eyes level*
Posture changes to alert	Posture unchanged
Preens, adjusts hair, attire	Does no preening
Turns body toward you	Turns body away
Tilts head	Head remains vertical
Narrows eyes slightly	Eyes remain normal
Twists, tugs at ring	Shows ring-back of hand
Smiles	Neutral, polite face
Matches your posture	Posture unchanged

Eyes sparkle	Normal or dull eyes
Licks her lips	*Keeps mouth closed*
Moves hand to her hip	*Posture unchanged*
Thrusts breasts	Sags to de-emphasize breasts

FROM ACROSS THE ROOM *In the first photo, she looks at the man she wants with a slight smile on her face. Notice that her wine glass is not directly in front of her as a barrier. Also notice that her empty hand is not gripping her knee, because that indicates getting hold of herself.*

In the second photo, she has looked at him again. She has removed her glasses (a barrier) and has barely tilted her head. Her smile is slightly bigger.

In the third photo, she has put her glass and her glasses down. Her posture has shifted from relaxed to erect and ready. She has turned so that her breasts face the man directly. Notice the open hand on her lap and uncrossed legs with feet flat on the floor—signs of openness and readiness. Finally, notice she is preening by checking her ear ring. That action also flashes her palm at the man.

SIDELONG GLANCE

Both men and women announce their interest by sneaking a peek. It begins with a look out of the corner of their eyes. The next time they look at you, they turn their head in your direction ever so slightly. The first sidelong glance is to see if you're worth looking at again. The second glance is to verify what they saw out of the corner of their eyes. When they look at you again, they are deciding if you are worth talking with.

LOOKS AT YOU A FEW TIMES

Both sexes follow sidelong glances by looking directly at the person a few times, but only for the socially appropriate length of time. They are verifying what they saw when sneaking a peek. The more often they look, the greater the interest. As with sidelong glances, they are still evaluating you.

HOLDS YOUR GAZE BRIEFLY

The person stares at you until you look at them, then they hold your gaze for longer than is socially appropriate. The way a *woman* breaks off this type of eye contact is significant.

DOWNCAST EYES

Women, if you are interested, look down before looking away. This your first act of submission and the first sign of reassurance that he will not be hurt if he comes over and talks with you.

Men, when you are the object of interest, after she has held your gaze long enough, give her a slight nod and a slight smile to acknowledge her existence then look away.

After breaking off, if the other person preens or changes posture to erect and ready, you have his, or her, interest. Shortly afterwards, if the person turns so the front of their body faces you when they are not looking in your direction, that's strong interest.

DOWNCAST EYES *After eye contact has been sustained for slightly longer than is socially appropriate, when the female looks down before she looks away, it is a solid sign of interest.*

This is a universal body language signal. Every culture, on every continent, features downcast female eyes as an early indicator of interest. It is one of the most reliable single gestures.

POSTURE CHANGES TO ERECT

When anyone becomes interested, they shift from casual and relaxed, to energized and erect, even when seated. This movement is among the most reliable single gestures. Although it's a slight change, you will notice if you are paying attention.

PREENING

After noticing someone attractive, we all adjust ourselves. Some common gestures: men fix their ties, women fluff their hair. Both sexes check their jewelry to be certain it is properly displayed. Quite reliable when following initial sustained eye-contact.

TILTS HEAD

When someone looks at you, holds your gaze briefly, then tilts their head, it means they are interested as well as seriously considering you. How-

ever, if a tilted head is not preceded by other signs
of interest, it usually signifies curiosity. A tilted
head during conversation is explained shortly.

TURNS BODY TOWARD YOU *The interested person turns toward you but does not look in your direction. This is a subconscious sexual display. The
woman shows off her breasts. The man shows off his
chest and shoulders, the source of his physical
power, as well presenting his genitals. Powerfully
reliable when following sustained eye contact and a
bit of preening.* **Moves Hand To Her Hip** *Usually
happens after she has turned her body to face you
and the two of you have exchanged signs of interest.
When she puts her hand on her hip, she is saying,
"Well, are you man enough to come over here?" Can
also be the opening move in a carefully orchestrated
game of Rapo.* **Thrusts Breasts** *Pulls her shoulders
back slightly so that her breasts are more noticeable.
Often precedes or follows hand-to-hip gesture. She's
saying, "Well, what do think of me?" Can also be
beginning of Rapo game.*

EYES NARROW SLIGHTLY

The interested person's eyes narrow slightly when looking at you. This sharpens focus and allows them to examine you carefully. Can happen anytime after they are done sneaking a peek at you. Reliable only when associated with other signs of interest. Could indicate poor vision rather than interest!

TUGS, TWISTS AT RING

Anyone wearing a ring signifying commitment sometimes will subconsciously pull or twist the ring if they become interested in you. They are not signaling you. They are making a symbolic attempt to lay aside the commitment while they court you.

SMILES

From across the room, any smile is good, a definite sign of interest. The best smile is *not* a big, broad, friendly smile even though that's a great beginning. The smile you want to see is a sensual one. The person's eyes are narrowed and their mouth is only slightly open so their teeth are only partially seen. Hard to miss! Extremely reliable when following any other signs of interest.

MATCHES YOUR POSTURE

People in the same emotional place, stand or sit in about the same posture. When someone changes posture to match yours, it probably means they are interested. A posture change usually happens after several signs of interest have been exchanged, but it can happen at any time. Reliable only when following other signs of interest.

EYES SPARKLE

Everyone's eyes sparkle when they are interested and excited. But, from across the room it is somewhat hard to notice. However, if you force yourself to focus on the other person's eyes, you can see this striking change as it takes place, even at a distance.

The shift usually takes place just after the person moves from relaxed to erect and ready. Extremely reliable no matter how difficult it is to notice.

LICKS HER LIPS

Sometimes done while she's preening. But usually happens after a sustained exchange of signals. It is a subconscious anticipation of your lips meeting. As with most other signs, reliable only when following other signals. Always used by *Rapo* players during each and every encounter.

CLUSTERS OF GESTURES

Believe only half of what you see, and none of what you hear, quoted at the beginning of this chapter is exactly right when you are trying to *see* what someone is nonverbally *saying*.

Study the picture in the first chapter titled *Major Cluster Of Gestures*. One gesture is not a message. One posture shift is not a message. One movement is not a message. Look for three or more signs of interest that appear in a cluster.

Men, for example, at a wedding reception, when your eyes first meet, she holds your gaze, narrows her eyes, shifts to a readiness posture, smiles, then looks down to break off eye contact. "Great!" is what you think. Whoa! Keep your pants on! Two clusters are better than one.

Here's what *really* happened. She's as vain as I am, so she doesn't wear her glasses. She thinks, "Damn! Is that obnoxious Hymen Ross?" as she squints slightly to see more clearly. Not sure, she gets ready to rush for the bathroom before he corners her, then feels guilty, gives a stiff smile and looks down, slightly ashamed.

One cluster of gestures cannot be relied on. To be certain of her interest, wait until you see another cluster. However, when she first shows interest, reciprocate with a cluster of your own. Shift your posture to erect, slightly narrow your eyes, then, after you look away, adjust your tie.

After a few minutes walk toward the group of people she is nearest to as if you are going to join them. With your peripheral vision, notice her body language as you get closer to her. She may relax when she realizes you're not Hymen Ross and then be awkward with embarrassment after realizing how vanity made her act like a fool.

No matter what happens as you approach the group, don't go over to her. Situate yourself where you can make further eye contact. Look in her direction now and then. Send another cluster of gestures. If she doesn't reciprocate, move on.

PRACTICE MAKES YOU AWARE

No matter where you are, the mall, a party, at the office, in a bar, make it a habit to study couples and small mixed groups. Become aware of the exchange of signals. Don't listen to words! Study what and how she's communicating and how he's responding.

Play a game with yourself or with a companion. Is the brunette in the blue dress interested in the guy wearing the Raiders cap? When he makes his move, figure out how she used her postures and gestures to get him to come over and talk with her.

Watch people until you're able to tell: (a) if he's interested in the woman across the room or the one he's talking with (b) how does she let him know he's supposed to come over and talk with her (c) how does she, or he, nonverbally announce the conversation is over?

Body Language Anecdote–Increase Your Awareness Twenty some years ago, in the midst of learning all about body language, I had a wonderful friend who was tall, skinny, extremely flat chested, pale and very plain looking. Beyond that, she loved dressing in second-hand store outfits that made her look even more gawky. But, at any party we both attended, guys who knew we were friends would corner me and want an introduction. The range extended from buttoned down, ex-corporate associates, to studly volleyball buddies and even a few undercover cop acquaintances!

Nancy was always somewhat surprised at her ability to attract men. One afternoon by the pool I offered to explain body language fundamentals so she could improve her batting average. Her reply was typical Nancy, "I don't want to know what I'm doing, 'cause I'll start analyzing and screw up whatever I'm doing right. Besides, that body language stuff is horseshit."

I never got to tell her, so I'll tell you what I observed about her unique ability to captivate. At every gathering she would begin to work her spell by being genuinely friendly with all of the women *first*.

She'd circulate, chatting and gossiping, joking and poking fun at sacred cows as she expounded her outrageous views on sex, men and politics. The effect— she neutralized most cattiness and competitiveness that could have been created later.

Fascinated, men watched her as she flowed from one end of the party to the other. What they saw was a woman who loved being female. Beyond that irresistible fundamental, they saw a woman who unashamedly enjoyed being sensual, and someone who relished being looked at with desire. But most of all, everyone, including me, saw a human being who loved being alive.

How did she communicate all that without a word? Body language.

In the beginning, when she charmed the women, Nancy used the same sexual signals and gestures an effeminate man would use. In short, when she was talking with an individual woman, she was also flirting with her.

But no matter which gender she was with, Nancy's most obvious body language was her energetic, erect and ready posture. As she chatted with one person, then another her head would tilt from one side, then to the other. Nancy touched anyone she was talking with for any reason as often as possible. And, she would smile the biggest smile and laugh the heartiest laugh over even the smallest incident.

When talking with just about everyone, her posture was always open. One hand would often be resting on her hip as the other hand held her drink low at her side. But, most of all, she made powerfully direct eye contact with everyone she looked at, even from afar. If that person was an interesting man, she'd smile and look down, then turn away with what we'd all describe as a little girl's shyness. Then almost immediately, she'd regain her womanliness and go back to her jubilant circulating.

If you know an average looking woman like Nancy who's skillful at attracting men, study her gestures and postures. Sooner or later, you'll realize how she does it. You can ask her, but I sincerely doubt if she can explain. It's something she learned intuitively as she was growing up by observing women in her life who were experts.

IN SUMMARY

Frequency of eye contact, the more the better. Amount of time he, or she, holds your gaze, the longer the better. How *she* breaks off eye contact, down before away is great! Shine of the eyes, the brighter the better. Direction of body, toward you, good. Overall posture, erect and alert are good. Tilt of head, vertical is bad. Where the drink is held, high as a barrier is bad. Hand activity, clenched, squeezing or pinching is bad but open, caressing or stroking is great.

AVOID FRUSTRATION AND ANGER

Please take a moment and read the *Preface* if you skipped it. Because, in it I presented the premise that underlies the entire book. Without reading the *Preface*, you may not enjoy, or learn, what is needed from *What Is Courtship?* the next chapter.

Also, please take a few seconds to read Darwin's quote at the beginning of the next chapter.

VIDEO CD of Body Language and Steel Balls Principles
When learning body language a single picture is worth 1000 words. When UNDERSTANDING body language a moving picture is worth 10,000 words. (1) saw pictures in book (2) saw in moving pictures at steelballs.com THE X SHOW (3) saw Titanium Babes in a video at the MOSB gathering (4) saw in the flesh at a bar/club at your last MOSB gathering . . . all serve as the FOUNDATION for what you are about to see AND really "GET." I devoted 100 hours editing the SFO Body Language video into this 2-VCD set. I cut it so the show moves. This video is INTENSE. These vcd's make it possible for you to get Body Language and many of the fundamental STEEL BALLS PRIN-CIPLES. There is a 20 minute review called MACHINE GUN SUM-MARY. Everything is compressed, thus AMPLIFIED. VCD is a format designed to STEAL movies and send them to third world countries. The quality is like a video tape. Don't expect a DVD! The information is something that nobody else on the planet has so it is virtually priceless. This 2-VCD set is only $49.

---

*In the most distinct classes of the animal
kingdom, with mammals, birds, reptiles
fishes, insects, and even crustaceans,
the difference between the sexes
follow almost exactly the same rules;
the males are always the wooers.*

CHARLES DARWIN, *The Descent of Man,* 1871

What Is Courtship?

Courtship is practiced by all species in which the
male is a beggar, that is, the female does not instinctively and actively seek copulation. Each species has a ritual that must be followed carefully. The
rituals involve displays of dominance and aggres-
siveness on the part of the male, reluctance and sub-
missiveness on the part of the female.

Adult gorillas take five hours to complete an in-
tricate dance of gestures and branch waving. That's
four hours longer than it takes to conduct the typical singles' bar ritual.

IT'S LOTS OF THINGS

Courtship is subtle. Courtship is demonstrating
good intentions. Courtship is signaling. Courtship is
nonverbal. Courtship is calming fears. Courtship is
attraction, supplication, stimulation, fascination,
exhilaration, inspiration, titillation, but most of all,
courtship is—PERSUASION.

In the animal world, the function of courtship is
to persuade the female to let the male mount and
penetrate her. Contrary to what many people want

to believe, we humans are animals. To be scientifically exact, we are:

PHYLUM	*CHORDATA*
CLASS	*VERTEBRATE*
ORDER	*MAMMAL*
FAMILY	*PRIMATE*
GENUS	*HOMO*
SPECIES	*SAPIENS.*

SELECTIVE FOR AGGRESSIVE

Females of every single species of mammal, except one, refuse to mate with non-aggressive males. That species is our own, homo sapiens. However, the aberration is rare. Females who will only mate with passive males cannot exist in nature any more than passive males can. Both are unnatural. NOTE 2

Men, you must be aggressive to get things underway. Then you have to slow down and court her. Just be your silly old self and have fun with her until she is persuaded. How do you know that you are persuading her? Be aware of her body language.

A MINI-SCENARIO OF COURTSHIP

You approach her, an act of aggression. She smiles, an act of reassurance. You smile back, an act of reassurance. You say or do something aggressive. In response, she says or does something submissive, aggressive or reassuring. The ball's in your court.

If she's aggressive it may be a test of your courage and worth, or she could be frightened and need to be reassured you intend no harm. Then again, she may want you to drop dead. Reluctance requires a bit more aggression. How much? Depends. Read on.

If she's submissive or has reassured you, don't respond with aggression. It's been established, at least for the moment, you're the dominant one. Show you won't hurt or embarrass her by being briefly submissive, a shy smile, a bit of boyish awkwardness.

Then be aggressive.

How aggressive? Depends. On what? Your ability to determine what's needed to be accepted as dominant without chasing her away.

Here's a simple act of aggression to test her level of interest. Briefly lean into her personal space under any pretense then back out. This is known as an "advance." If she leans away, you're not welcome, at least not yet. But if she holds her ground, further advances may soon be welcome.

AN EXPERT'S PERSPECTIVE

In an interview with *Bottom Line*, Diane Ackerman, Ph.D., naturalist and author of *A Natural History of Love* answered these questions:

What are the basic conflicts that produce differences between men and women?

Many of them stem from competing biological agendas that have been passed along from earliest time. Men have always been driven to impregnate as many women as possible in order to ensure the existence of future generations.

A woman's investment in reproduction has always been far more demanding. Pregnancy makes her physically vulnerable, and once she gives birth, she makes great sacrifices to ensure the survival of her child and herself. She also expects one man to stick by her, helping at least until the baby is born and safely on its feet

To apply this to contemporary life, men are naturally inclined to avoid being tied down, whereas women are more likely to think about relationships in terms of *always, forever* and *commitment.*

Why haven't some of these attitudes changed as society has changed?

Relative to human history, civilization happened in the blink of an eye. Men and women today may be wearing suits and carrying briefcases, but we still respond to the same instincts and concerns that we developed over eons of time. Though our *instincts* have not changed, our *expectations* have.

To make matters even more complicated, we are constantly bombarded by images of perfect relationships in movies, on TV and in advertisements. Therefore, we measure ourselves against an impossible criteria.

There is much more information on how our animal nature influences us during courtship. However, that topic does not belong here. It will distract us. For those interested, in *natural sex,* see NOTE 3 in the Appendix.

The next stage is to open courtship negotiations (persuade her) by following the *Commandments Of Meeting.*

NOTE 2
There are passive men and there are women who seek them. They are part of the courtship and dating universe. See *ABNORMAL HAPPENS* in the Appendix to find out why some people are not capable of taking part in a normal, natural man-woman relationship.

NOTE 3
Once we understand how much of our behavior is *not* subject to our will power, it is far easier to relax and enjoy the timeless, wonderful rituals of courtship. See *SEX IS NUM-BER FOUR* in the Appendix.

*Once negotiations begin
it's only a matter of time before castle walls
crumble or maidenhead breached.*

CHURCHILL

Commandments
Of Meeting

As stated in the *Preface*, on most occasions, the man must do something to get things started. So, men, here are the facts. Nearly every woman you approach wants the same things.

SEVEN THINGS WOMEN WANT

(1) Don't be pushy, I'm not good at telling people to buzz off.

(2) Don't be obvious, although I may be interested, I don't want everyone to know.

(3) Even if this is fun and exciting, I may be a bit nervous.

(4) Don't show you're nervous, it makes me nervous. Be casual, friendly and relaxed. It'll help me stay that way.

(5) Keep the conversation superficial, further into it, leave a few openings for me to tactfully indicate if I want to continue or not.

(6) Later on, when I'm more sure of myself, don't ask for too much. Give me room to maneuver to save face, mine and yours.

(7) If I turn you down, don't act like a jerk because you started this.

ON NOT BEING DIRECT

Everyone communicates obliquely during the early stages of courtship. If you're straightforward it throws off the other person's timing as well as disorienting her, or him, as well as making the person feel you're not playing by the rules. Forget "communication skills" you learned from your marriage counselor or therapist. They are completely ineffective in the single world.

At a minimum, direct talk makes others think you're out of it, or crazy. After a few dates, when you're comfortable with each other, you can gradually start being more to the point, but in the beginning, indirect exchange of information is the only way to proceed.

Many single people are not direct for two reasons: (1) it protects them from the humiliation of rejection if the other person isn't interested and, (2) indirectness makes it possible to use the other person without risk of involvement.

Everyone is a suspected game player. Everyone is trying to protect himself or herself. Hey, too bad, that's how it really is. I didn't make the rule everybody's playing by—*All's fair in love and war.*

COURTSHIP BY CONVERSATION

We humans conduct courtship by talking. The complex but mandatory, ritualistic displays of dominance and submission, aggression, reluctance and reassurance all take place during conversation. Although the words you choose are important, even critical, most communicating is done with facial expression, tone of voice, posture and the manner of touching.

SAFETY FIRST

Men, as the aggressor, the first thing you must do is deliver an opening line that won't scare her away and won't make her think you're a playboy or a bumpkin. The next thing you have to do is sustain the conversation for a few minutes so that she can realize you are first of all *safe*, next, *interesting* and finally, *attractive*.

All women are afraid that any man who approaches them, including you, may be physically dangerous as well as socially or emotionally dangerous.

Physical Danger. She thinks you could be The Slasher or a Dirty Old Man trying to cop a feel. Convince her you're safe by keeping your distance, physically. Absolutely do not touch her except to shake hands. Your body language must *not* say lust, fear-of-rejection, impatience, or lack-of-confidence. During the entire conversation, even if you're petrified, you must *appear* to be friendly, relaxed and casual so that she has time to realize you are safe.

Social Danger. The woman you approach does not want everyone in the room to realize you are coming on to her. Why? If after talking with her for a few minutes, you decide she's not that interesting and walk away, everyone will know. Nobody wants to be humiliated in public. To save face, do not be obvious or up front. Your words as well as your body language must say, "I'm relaxed. We're just having a friendly, casual chat."

Emotional Danger. A woman is afraid you might be able to sexually use her, then discard her. Once she realizes you are not physically or socially dangerous, this is her biggest fear. Communicate nonverbally that you are sincere as well as trustworthy and not a playboy. This is done with postures, gestures, tone of voice and eye contact as explained. For the courtship to proceed, you must reassure her that you are not emotionally dangerous as the need arises. How will you know when? By paying close attention to her body language.

IN THE BEGINNING

She's afraid of the same things you are—being used, humiliated or rejected during courtship. She has her pride, just as you do. She can't respond directly to your advances without risking rejection by you. You could just be flirting or playing *Cavalier*. If she comes back with openness and receptivity you might laugh at her for taking you seriously.

To convince her you're safe, interesting and attractive, you must be yourself, at your best, of course.

To be successful, you must religiously follow the *Eleven Commandments Of Meeting*. You can't break even one!

THE ELEVEN COMMANDMENTS OF MEETING

    I. *Thou shalt not start out hard*

   II. *Thou shalt not look at her breasts or buns*

  III. *Thou shalt not mention the ex or children*

  IV. *Thou shalt not look at other females*

   V. *Thou shalt not talk over or down to her*

  VI. *Thou shalt not be slick and smooth*

 VII. *Thou shalt not be negative or cynical*

VIII. *Thou shalt not mention sex*

  IX. *Thou shalt not ask about boyfriends*

   X. *Thou shalt not touch, except to shake hands*

  XI. *Thou shalt not reveal a standing interest in her.*

To be successful, pay attention to what is being said with, and without, words. Although the next chapter is written principally for men, assertive women can do the same things as the two of you have your first *Conversations Without Words*.

So, thru the eyes, love attains the heart
For the eyes are the scouts of the heart
And the eyes go reconnoitering for
What it would please the heart to possess.
And when they are in full accord, firm
All in one resolve, at that time,
Perfect love is born from what the eyes
Have made welcome to the heart.

12th century troubadour's song
JOSEPH CAMPBELL, *THE POWER OF MYTH*

Just one look, that's all it took.
DORIS TROY, 1956

Conversations Without Words

Most of us are slightly afraid as well as somewhat excited in settings where social interaction is expected and required. So, most people do not sit or stand in an *open* posture. But, during courtship, the more open the other person's posture is, the more open that person is to you and your advances.

OPEN AND CLOSED

If you're wide open while sitting, your posture is similar to Abe Lincoln's in the Lincoln Memorial. Your feet are flat on the floor. Your hands are relaxed, not clenching anything. And, you're not holding a drink in front of yourself as a symbolic barrier.

While standing, you're open when your hands are *not* in your pockets. You are *not* leaning against anything. Your feet are flat on the floor. And, your drink is *not* in front of you.

OPEN AND CLOSED *When the person's posture is open, he's open to you, your ideas, and possibly your advances. In the left photo, notice that although he's smiling, he is gripping his knee tightly indicating he's controlling himself. Also notice the beer can is held high in front as a barrier. In the right picture, both feet are firmly planted on the ground indicating he is sincere. Notice that his arms are down and that his hands are open and relaxed, signs of openness and sincerity. His head is slightly tilted and he's leaning a bit forward. Both indicate interest.*

MIRROR, MIRROR

This topic applies to a man approaching and interacting with a woman just as it obviously applies the other way 'round. In body language jargon, it's called *mirroring*.

If you're in the same emotional place as the other person, your posture is the mirror image theirs. It also can mean that you are interested in each other.

MIRRORING *These people are sitting in almost exactly the same position, so they are about in the same place emotionally. But, notice she's holding onto her shin and does not have her foot completely flat on the floor. The man must take his time until she's more open and relaxed.*

When you notice the other person is standing or sitting in about the same manner as you are, he, or she, is in about the same emotional place. During courtship, *subconsciously*, all of us tend to adopt the same posture as the person we are interested in.

When talking with someone we are attracted to, we usually mirror them. More fascinating, we often mirror somebody we are interested even if that person is across the room and we are stuck talking with a bore! One more time. *You cannot not communicate.*

RAISE YOUR AWARENESS

Pay attention when you are at a party. Lots of

people always gather in the kitchen. Look around. Notice if anyone is mirroring another person's body language. They may be interested in each other, then again, they could simply be in the same emotional state. Look for other signals to confirm or deny the interest you suspect. At the same time, *consciously* adopt the body language of the person you'd like to meet and talk with.

FIRST CONVERSATION SIGNALS

Men, pay attention to all the ways she communicates during the first few minutes as you talk with her. Women, let him know what you want.

Nearly all of these signals apply to both men and women. The ones that apply only to women are indicated by *italics*.

KEEP TALKING	MOVE ON
Alert, energetic	Tense, restless
Pupils dilated	Normal or small pupils
Gradually opens posture	Posture remains closed
Lowers drink	Keeps drink high
Touches self gently	Grips or pinches self
Caresses objects	Squeezes, taps objects
Crosses and uncrosses legs	*Legs remain crossed*
Flashes of palm	*Back of hand gestures*
Crossed legs steady	Swings crossed legs
Dangles shoe on toe	*Keeps shoe on*
Hands never touch face	Touches face
Touches you any reason	*Never touches you*
Feet firmly on floor	Feet on edges or toes
Loosens anything	Tightens anything
Leans forward	Leans away
Steady hands, feet	Tapping, drumming

ALERT, ENERGETIC

Ready for action with you. Contrast with relaxed, casual postures when sitting or standing. Especially positive and revealing when the person shifts from casual to alert during the conversation.

GRADUALLY OPENS POSTURE

In social settings, most of us start out in a closed, defensive posture because we're a bit apprehensive. A closed posture *feels* safe. When the person you are talking with shifts to a more open posture, it signifies trust and comfort. That person is, literally, opening up to you and what you have to offer.

LOWERS DRINK

Most people in social settings hold a drink in front of themselves as a barrier. When the person you are talking with lowers his, or her, drink, the barrier between you is coming down. As always, it is most effective if you lower your drink first. The other person often follows your lead.

CARESSES OBJECTS

If done sensually, it usually means the person wants to caress you or wants you to caress them.

CARESSING A GLASS *The most common object fondled is a drink. Women tend to stroke the glass up and down. Men usually run a finger around the lip. The symbolism is obvious.*

Caution! Occasionally, when a woman touches something sensitively, it can be a subtle signal for reassurance. Subconsciously, she may want you to gently reassure her. You may be too close physically or you're talking about a topic that makes her anxious. Move back and change the subject if you read this gesture as nervousness.

TOUCHES HERSELF

If done in a gentle, sensuous manner it means the same as caressing an object—the person wants to touch you or wants you to touch them. However, this can also be an attempt at reassuring one's self. It depends on everything that came before. The same caution as above applies.

FLASHES OF PALM She shows you the palm of her hand during conversation in brief flashes. She is making herself submissive and vulnerable. One interpretation is, "My hands are up. I surrender." Another way of seeing it, "I have no weapon. I won't hurt you."

PALM FLASH

Women only. She shows you the palm of her hand during conversation while checking her ear ring or adjusting her hair or gesturing with her hands. This signal is hard to see because it is so brief and it does not appear to be flirting.

Reliable if you can notice it. Focus your awareness on looking for palm flashes ahead of time and you'll be able to see it or the opposite gesture, described in the photo below.

BACK OF HAND *Women only. The exact opposite of a palm flash. One interpretation is "See my wedding ring? I'm not interested." Another is "This is not a fist, yet. Beat it!" Often disguised, as in the photo.*

CROSSES AND UNCROSSES LEGS

Women only. When sitting with a skirt on, she's flashing a bit of thigh to entice you. When sitting with pants on, she is subconsciously doing the same thing. However, when standing, she is probably just be trying to get comfortable or it may indicate she's excited and ready to go.

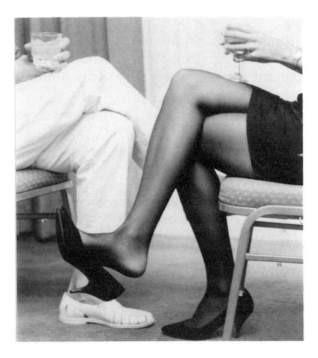

DANGLES SHOE ON TOE *Women only. When sitting with her legs crossed, she wiggles her heel out of the shoe, then lets the shoe dangle on her toes. Opening up and loosening up to you. It's a subconscious first step in disrobing.*

STEADY HANDS, FEET, LEGS

Stable means relaxed, not reluctant or hesitant. When feeling negative emotions, both men and women fidget, tap or drum something. As mentioned, females are taught to sit still. Consider that when interpreting a woman's wiggling feet.

LOOSENS ANYTHING

Loosening up to you. It can be unbuttoning, unzipping or untying. A man loosens his tie for the same reason that a women lets her shoe dangle on her toes. It's symbolic disrobing.

LEANS FORWARD

This simple gesture says all of this: *You have my attention. I want to hear what you have to say. I want to see you more clearly. I want to be closer to you.* Very powerful and very reliable.

SHE TOUCHES YOU ANY REASON

Touching is possession or to verify what one sees. When she touches you, even "accidentally" she's interested. Men, keep your hands to yourself until she touches you.

Attention Men! No matter where, when or how a woman touches you, it is a strong signal of interest. Women often "accidentally" touch a man they are interested in as they make their way to the bar or rest room.

Caution! Women who are *Rapo* players touch men early and often. Men who touch women before the women touch them are probably manipulators and liars, as mentioned.

HANDS NEVER TOUCH FACE

As mentioned, when someone touches himself above the neck, it usually means he's lying or he doesn't believe what you are saying.

FEET FIRMLY ON FLOOR

Feet that are solidly grounded mean the person is taking a stand, is not reluctant or hesitant. However, feet that are not solidly grounded usually mean trouble ahead.

COMING FROM THE SAME PLACE

People who are in different emotional states don't enjoy talking with each other. For example, if you are bold and confident and I'm nervous, I won't be able to relax and be pleasant, thus you won't enjoy talking with me. The End. So, you must *appear* to be in about the same place as the person you are attempting to court.

Men, if her posture is open, that's good. Match her posture and remain open as you talk.

If her posture is closed, match her posture, then as you are conversing, gradually open up, one small step at a time. If she doesn't follow your first few shifts toward openness, stop. She's not ready or is not interested.

When there are good vibrations between the two of you, adapt you posture to match hers and wait a few more minutes before trying to slowly open up again.

While you are slowly moving from a closed position to an open position, she has time to realize that you are not dangerous and could be interesting. Only after she has discovered (1) that you are safe and (2) interesting, can she find you attractive.

MOVE FROM CLOSED TO OPEN *The series of photos on the next page show you what to do if the other person is not in an open posture. Although this example shows a man going first and becoming vulnerable, women can do the same thing.*

First adjust your stance so that your posture approximates hers. As you talk, gradually and carefully shift your posture to a more open position, one step at a time. Subconsciously, the other person often follows your lead and "opens up to you" because you made yourself vulnerable first. In the top photo, the man has adopted the same posture as the woman. In the middle photo, he has moved from completely closed to semi-open by uncrossing his arms and putting his hands in his pockets. In the bottom photo, he has become completely vulnerable by putting his hands behind himself. She has mirrored his posture.

When women adopt this position, it causes their breasts to protrude slightly, which commands the man's attention. Also, when women stand in this position, they appear to be slightly submissive, thus safe.

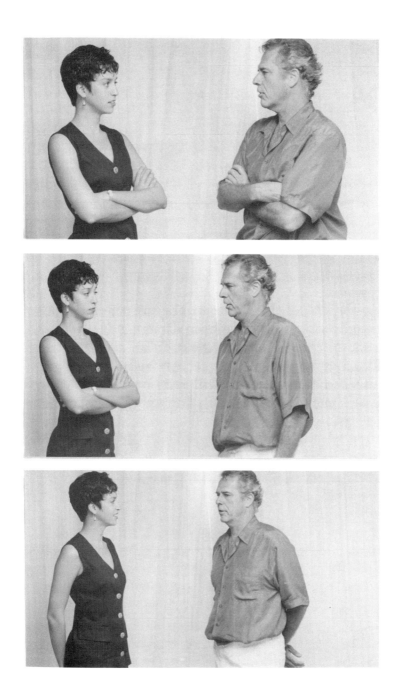

*FROM CLOSED TO OPEN AND BEYOND In the
sequence of photos on the next page, you can see many
signs of interest.*

*Overall, as the two are talking, the woman moves
from a closed posture to an open posture.*

*Study the photos carefully and you can notice that
the man mirrors her actions.*

*The encounter begins with her arms crossed and
with her ankles locked under the chair. As the conversation continues, she unlocks her ankles and puts
her feet flat on the floor, sits up and leans toward the
man. Next she uncrosses her arms. Notice that her
hands are open and relaxed as she leans even closer.*

*In the last photo, she is touching herself gently in a
sensuous way.*

At the end of the first conversation, many subtle
and indirect signals have been exchanged. However,
during *Further Conversations Without Words,* the
next chapter, more nonverbal signals are exchanged. Some of them will still be subtle. Many
will be somewhat obvious. But a few will be blatant!

Charm is how one gets the answer 'Yes' without asking any clear question.
ALBERT CAMUS

Further Conversations Without Words

It makes no difference how much time has passed, five minutes or five hours, since the first conversation. Your subconscious will have processed much of the nonverbal information the two of you exchanged. That makes it possible for you to *see* more clearly what the other person is *saying* during later conversations

During the second conversation, stronger signals are exchanged as the man continues his effort to persuade and the woman continues her effort to determine his worthiness. Many of the gestures and signs from the first conversation are used but new ones are added. Some signals are so important, they are repeated here.

Nearly all of these signals apply to both men and women. However, this chapter is written as though the woman is sending and the man receiving.

YOU'RE DOING GREAT!	ONLY BEING POLITE
Keeps eyes on you	Looks around room
Head tilts farther	Head only slightly tilted
Smiles broadly and often	Smiles slightly
Hands open, relaxed	Hands closed

Puts anything in mouth	Nothing goes in mouth
Posture changes to yours	Maintains posture
Turns body toward you	Keeps body facing away
Sucks straw, looks at you	*Looks away and drinks*
Removes eyeglasses	Puts on eyeglasses

KEEPS EYES ON YOU

During conversation, the other person is focused on you, not looking around the room, at the dancers on the floor, the band or at anything other than you. Reliable if accompanied by other signs of interest.

HEAD TILTS FARTHER

A tilted head usually indicates interest but it also can mean the person is curious. When the person's head tilts even more, it indicates even more interest or curiosity.

REMOVES EYEGLASSES *Usually means the person is lowering the barrier that prevents you from looking deeply into the windows of their soul. Similar but stronger than lowering a drink held up as a barrier. However, it can indicate a refusal to "see" you or what you are saying. Notice the open hands with palms up gesture. This indicates sincerity and openness.*

UNCROSSES LEGS, ARMS

The person is opening up to you and your advances! Extremely reliable if the openness is maintained. Crossed arm and crossed legs indicate a closed mind or a closed heart, or both.

POSTURE CHANGES TO YOURS

The person's emotions are changing to match yours when they adopt a posture similar to yours. That's unless they've read *Mirroring* in this book!

SUCKS STRAW, LOOKS AT YOU Doesn't get much more blatant unless she also licks her lips. The symbolism is obvious.
Caution! Women who play Rapo use this gesture all the time. Unless she was a bit nervous at the outset, then gradually relaxed, this gesture is probably a game player's move.

TURNS BODY TOWARD YOU

Powerful signal! Indicates a strong interest and attraction. She's displaying her womanliness and making herself vulnerable to you.

SMILES BROADLY AND OFTEN

During conversation, a broad smile indicates the person is enjoying the interaction with you. Slight smiles or no smiles indicate serious, intense interest or no interest at all.

HANDS OPEN, RELAXED

Open hands indicate openness to you. Clenched hands indicate fear or anger. Holding tightly to anything, the arm of the chair, one's own leg, even one's wine glass, is literally, *holding on* to one's emotions, controlling one's self. The emotion held back could be anything from sexual excitement or utter suspicion. It's usually fear of rejection or fear of being humiliated.

PUTS ANYTHING IN MOUTH

Sometime done by a man, but usually a woman does this. As with touching herself sensually, it indicates she wants to put *you* into her mouth. This action must be sensual. If not, she's probably trying to reassure herself with a symbolic baby's pacifier. When biting accompanies it, anger is just below the surface.

REASSURANCE REQUIRED

Most women don't respond directly to you and your advances until they feel confident about their own attractiveness and your motives. Usually, a woman's defenses are up during early conversations. If she experiences any of this as too dangerous, she'll take flight physically or emotionally.

There's a thin line between being an aggressive male and being too much for her. The less confidence she has, the less aggressive you must be while still being assertive.

Caution, Men! You cannot rely on her face to tell you when she needs to be reassured. Women are taught that they must never offend others during social intercourse. So, nearly all women continue to smile and keep their faces pleasant appearing even when they are becoming uncomfortable. Here's how she lets you know that you are *not* persuading her.

YOU'RE COMING ON TOO STRONG

Averts her eyes	Looks around room
Nervous smile	Touches her face or head
Leans or backs away	Turns front of body away
Touches throat, necklace	Picks at hand or finger
Moves head to vertical	Hands begin to clench, grip
Begins to fidget	Raises drink in front of her

When you notice any, even one, of these signs, move back physically. You may be standing or sitting too close. You may be leaning into her territory too far or too often. If you touched her, even in a socially appropriate way, such as admiring her ring or bracelet, it was probably too soon and possibly fatal!

TOUCHES MOUTH, EYES OR EARS

When the person is listening—*Touches Mouth* means I don't believe you or I don't want say something rude. *Touches Eye*—I can't see what you are saying or I don't like looking at you. *Touches Ear*—I don't believe what I'm hearing or I don't want to hear what you have to say.

If the person is talking—*Touches Mouth* means I don't believe what I'm saying or I'm hesitant to say this. *Touches Eye*—I don't want to look at you when I'm lying or I'm so excited or scared or confused, I don't want you to look into my eyes. *Touches Ear*—I can't believe what I'm saying. These gestures were explained in detail and illustrated with photos earlier in *Lines, Lies Or The Truth*.

LEANS OR BACKS AWAY

This means that you are too close physically or emotionally. Hard to notice because most people do not want to appear rude, so they only lean back a little. Could indicate you have bad breath.

The topic of your conversation may be inappropriate. Change subjects to something light and pleasant. It is also possible that she thinks you are a complete jerk.

When you spot two of these gestures in a row, it's time to excuse yourself and circulate before you destroy your chances forever.

TOUCHES THROAT, NECKLACE Only women. *Means that she is trying to prevent herself from backing up or leaning away. Her hand and forearm serve as a barrier. You have offended her with the topic or your language or you are too close physically or emotionally.*

Here are the gestures she, or he, uses to tell you that you have crossed the line and now you should move on.

THAT'S ENOUGH, GO AWAY!

Looks away often	Shifts posture, turns away
Becomes tense	Stops smiling, starts frowning
Brushes imaginary lint	Sits up straight
Crosses arms, legs	Picks up drink
Locks ankles under chair	Hands close, clench

Drums fingers, swings leg, taps foot.

RAISES OR PICKS UP DRINK

The person is replacing the barrier that was lowered or set aside. This shuts you out.

BRUSHES AWAY IMAGINARY LINT *Gives you "the brush off," literally. Also seen when the person is, disbelieving, angry, bored. It can also mean that the person believes he is vastly superior to a piece of lint like you.*

RHYTHMIC MOTIONS

Finger drumming, toe tapping, swinging leg, leg bouncing up and down on tip of toe, using swizzle stick or anything else as a drumstick (club) and all other such movement indicates the person is disinterested, bored, impatient, nervous or angry.

HANDS CLOSE, CLENCH INTO FISTS

Closing up emotionally and closing you out. Usually indicates anger. The person may be subconsciously getting ready to hit you.

CROSSES ARMS, LEGS

The person is closing you out physically which closes you out emotionally. As mentioned before, can also indicate a closed mind.

LOCKS ANKLES UNDER CHAIR Similar to clenching one's hands and crossing one's legs or arms. You are being closed out. Can also be an attempt at controlling one's emotions, usually fear but if other signs are positive the person is controlling excitement.

Body Language Anecdote–You Cannot Not Communicate In 1982, I was recently divorced and naive about the single's world. (That's redundant, of course.) So, my two best friends took me to the ruling pick-up club for some on-the-job training.

The parking lot was packed. As we drove around looking for a parking place, I kept muttering, "Don't like the vibes. Bad vibes at this place!" Mark replied, "Get real! We're not even inside yet! You can't possibly feel anything!"

Disco was in its death throes most places, but in the heart of Orange County, it was "staying alive." Once inside, my friends took off for the bar and left me staring at a scene I found surreal.

The women were 22-42, blond and attractive or non-blonde and attractive. To my amazement, many actually were dressed like disco dollies. You know, five hours in the making. Men were mostly 30-50, business types and a few Middle Eastern career students.

I was transfixed. The music roared as billions of attractive females floated by, just a few inches from my face.

Suddenly, Disco Dick appeared, violating the scene. I stared. My God! Just like in *Saturday Night Fever,* he was wearing gold chains, black patent leather platform shores, a bright red satin shirt open to the navel and skin tight black pants held up by a chrome belt.

He grabbed a tall blonde by the wrist, spun her around until she was facing him and pointed. She nodded and they sauntered toward the dance floor.

I was dumbfounded. Why didn't she smack him? Manhandling her like that! How could she then dance with such a maggot? What the hell is going on?

My friends appeared. Each handed me a beer and

motioned for me to follow. We ended up on a wide, raised walkway that ringed the dance floor. To be heard, John shouted in my ear, "We can check out the women from here." I nodded.

After a few minutes, I pointed to the blonde on the dance floor and yelled in John's ear. He shrugged, gesturing he couldn't hear me, but looked where I pointed. One bit of music blended into another. Disco Dick went his way. As the blonde walked by us, she slowed down, gave me the head to toe once over and kept going.

I backed up and leaned hard against the wall. And, even with a beer in each hand, I crossed my arms across my chest. Both friends looked at her, then at me, then at the way I was standing. They stared at one another, each with a puzzled expression.

The music was roaring as John pointed, pulled on my arm and pointed again. I didn't know what he wanted. I shrugged. He pulled harder. So, I leaned against the wall harder and crossed my arms even harder.

He looked at Mark and signaled. Mark grabbed my other arm and they both pulled me away from the wall but I kept my arms crossed. They spun me around and pushed me toward the men's room.

Inside, they both wanted to know—Why don't you go ask that blonde to dance? What the hell is the matter with you? Why are you standing like that?

With my arms still rigidly crossed, I indignantly pronounced, "If she'd dance with scum like that, I wouldn't even talk with her!"

They both howled, then spent five minutes trying to convince me that just because a woman dances with a slime ball it doesn't mean anything. My arms remained crossed and my mind remained closed, as it does to this day.

A few weeks later, I remembered my impressions of "bad vibrations" in the parking lot. I threw it in Mark's face. Although he ridiculed "that psychological gibberish," I forever lost all doubt that no matter what, *you cannot not communicate*, even at 50 yards!

The next chapter, *On Shaking Hands,* explains why the handshake is the quickest, most reliable method to discover who's who. Shake with everyone. It gives you the advantage.

The first attraction was purely physical.

ROD STEWART

Touch me, feel me.

THE WHO, 1979

On Shaking Hands

The touching that takes place when shaking hands enables your emotions and subconscious to make lightning fast value judgements. The power of touch bypasses the logical, rational brain and becomes hard evidence.

Massive amounts of genuine data are exchanged as the two of you touch in this socially acceptable manner. What you both learn is gut knowledge—reliable and accurate as to who the other person *really* is.

WOMEN FIRST

Women, remember, you have a tremendous advantage during this data exchange—your intuition. Trust it! Use it!

By touching, you are able to fill your brain with authentic, trustworthy information as to what he's all about. And, you are able to send him just about any nonverbal message you want. That's how powerful a woman *can be* if she chooses to use her natural abilities.

If the man does not offer his hand, extend yours. Keep your palm perpendicular to the floor, not slightly up, not slightly down. Smile politely, not sweetly. Grasp his hand completely and firmly, not with just your fingertips. Look him right in the eyes, and use his name, "Nice to meet you, Bernie." Shake firmly and let go. If he's whacko macho on this issue and is offended, it's much better to know it now.

Also, heed the advice given to men, below, regarding eye contact and making yourself briefly vulnerable as you shake hands.

SEPARATE THE WOMEN FROM THE GIRLS

Want to attract men who like cute, delicate little things? If not, get rid of your lady-like handshake. That's when you offer your fingertips, tilt your head, smile demurely and do a barely noticeable mini-curtsy.

To attract and interest someone who wants a woman, not a girl, you need a firm handshake. Have your manly friends coach you until the first impression you create is that you are a strong, interesting person, who happens to be female.

Some macho men, and men from the old school, don't want a woman who is an equal, so they offer their hand with the palm facing slightly down. That's their way of getting on top.

When you notice this ploy, don't turn your palm up to meet his! It makes you submissive from the beginning, not a good start. Extend your hand toward him but keep your palm perpendicular with the floor. Stop short! Don't reach out all the way. Pause and hold it there. Make him reach for you. This establishes your equality.

NOW FOR THE MEN

Men, shaking a woman's hand when you meet her makes you different from all boys, most young men, and many men who merely nod and smile when meeting her. She immediately puts you in a different category, Gentleman.

She can't deceive your stomach and you're a fool to ignore its judgement of her. While shaking her hand, look into her eyes and, for a few seconds, be vulnerable. Let her see you. See into her. It confirms or denies your other impressions of her. If you know what she's really like, as opposed to what she appears to be, you're way ahead of any competition. So, you can adjust your courtship approach and pace accordingly.

Although some women are a bit disoriented when you offer your hand, they quickly recover and reciprocate. Sometimes it's in a submissive manner. Sometimes as an equal. Sometimes as the opening move in a game of *Rapo*. Now and then, like a dead end bore.

I've saved myself far more than the price of a drink by excusing myself at the earliest opportunity after shaking hands. I'm not interested in game players or teases. One sophisticated looking beauty turned out to be nothing but a shy, frightened doe. Not my type at all. On a few occasions, I skipped ninety percent of the preliminaries based only on the sparks that flew when we grasped each other in this socially acceptable manner.

Warning To Men! You must have a firm, masculine hand shake. If you don't, develop one. Get advice from your guy friends. You don't have to say what you're practicing for. Feedback is necessary to change.

The next chapter is how you go about *Meeting Ms Or Mr Right* at social gatherings and meetings. All that's necessary is a bit of courage *after* you know the other person is somewhat interested in you. Although it's written from a man's point of view (I'm a man), the strategy and methods work even better for women!

*There is no such thing as luck,
only preparation meeting opportunity.*
COACH LOMBARDI

Meeting Ms Or Mr Right

What to do after the two of you have exchanged mild signs of interest from across the room? The next step is to have a one-word conversation.

Acknowledge her every time you have the chance. Say "Hi," nod and smile on your way to, or from the men's room, bar, kitchen or pool. You're just being friendly. These "Hi's" are first conversations. You won't be a stranger when you start the second conversation.

You want to know, *How and when do I do that?* Right? I don't mean to be glib, but it depends on the situation and it depends on how strong the signals were.

Since the variations are infinite, let's just get two things straight, okay? First, the only time a man gets rejected is when he approaches a woman who is *not* interested in him. Second, after signs of interest have been exchanged, then followed up with a couple of nods, smiles and a "Hi," nothing bad can happen, no matter what you do. She wants to, and will, talk with you, period.

The information and techniques presented in the next few pages are examples from the real world of R. Don Steele.

HAPPY SOCIAL OCCASIONS

Here are the answers to the *How* and *When* questions from above.

At Mike's annual Summer Solstice party, Margie and I had mild, sustained eye contact from time to time. Later, I nodded and smiled as she passed by on her way to the powder room. I moved into the kitchen and waited for her to come by.

When she did, all I said was, "Hi. I'm Mike's volleyball friend, Don," and offered my hand which she shook enjoyably then smiled but only said, "Hi, Margie," and stood there. I recovered quickly and added, "You work at Mike's office?" She didn't, so we exchanged the obligatory information about what we did and where we worked then moved into an enjoyable exchange of office politics stories and complaints. During it all, we held another conversation without words.

> *Helpful Hint.* At all gatherings, never park yourself for long any place. Circulate. If you must stop for awhile, remember that at all parties, sooner or later, everyone passes through the kitchen. It's a great place to watch the body language as you watch the traffic.

Jean, at a wedding reception, after good eye contact on and off for half an hour, I noticed that now and then she was eavesdropping on some of my conversations. When the opportunity presented itself, I butted into one of her conversations with, "Get all the grants you can. Lie on the application if you have to. It's your money. You'll pay it all back to the bastards in taxes sooner or later."

That led to a discussion of the strategy behind

business proposal writing, which I did for a living, versus proposal grant writing. From there we moved on to our mutual dislike of the Dallas Cowboys. What can I say? Once engaged in verbal intercourse, things often get pleasantly out of hand!

STRAIGHTFORWARD ON YOUR OWN

At social gatherings, people stand around in small groups talking. The woman you want to meet is often in one. Trouble is, unless you know someone in that group, it's damn near impossible to be invited to join it. Here's how to increase the probability that you will know someone in her group.

At a fund-raising reception, chamber of commerce mixer, or any party where you don't know very many people, she's going to be gone in only a few hours, so you must get everything started immediately.

Nod, smile and say a friendly "Hi!" to each and every person you see from the time you park the car until you're situated where you can look the place over. You're building a foundation to work from.

This simple action gives you the excuse and the chance to say later on to several people, "Hi! Yeah, saw you on the way in. I'm Don. Work with Jim" Or, "Friend of the candidate." Or, "Went through finance training with Jenene, the Vice President."

Get everything going quickly by using this line to introduce yourself and have brief conversations with as many different people as possible. You're setting it up to meet *her*. Keep it short and move on. The more people you meet the better your chances are. It makes no difference what sex or how old.

When you see her talking with one of the people you "met" by saying, "Hi! I'm Don . . ." you'll be able to join their group. Conversation with her will naturally follow. In fact, you'll probably be introduced to each other!

Plus, it's much easier for any woman interested in you to join a group you are in because she may know someone. Once she joins your group, you'll probably be introduced to each other. Got it?

CLASS OR CLUB MEETING

The principles are the same as meeting her as described above. But, she's going to be there next week and the week after that, so take it easy. Let her know you're aware of her existence and acknowledge it. Just say "Hi." Don't appear to be anything but friendly and slightly interested. Be discreet in front of everyone.

Let her become used to you. Get to know other people first. She'll feel less threatened if three or four people are going to the student union for coffee at break or to the restaurant after the meeting.

Get on the same subcommittee or class project without being blatantly noticeable. When the situation is right, under any pretext, ideally class or club related, start the second conversation. Remember to shake her hand and introduce yourself a few minutes into it.

After a few minutes of talk, compliment her on anything you genuinely like or admire about her, especially her clothing and accessories. This must be genuine or you immediately dismissed as a bullshit artist.

Praising something she picked out, like a bracelet or shoes is best. Every man tells her she has beautiful eyes or whatever. You're different. Only one compliment per conversation, because you have The Right Attitude. More later.

GETTING NOTICED–PART I

This method, dubbed, "The Photographer Ploy," is useful for meeting someone you noticed but she hasn't noticed you. I stumbled on this when I volunteered to take informal shots at a friend's wedding.

Most people like to have their pictures taken, no matter how much they protest. Have a camera with you at all light-hearted gatherings. Don't be an obvious twit and only take photos of the women. Shoot lots of pictures of everyone. It gives you a chance to meet and talk with even more guests.

When she's in a shot, ask her, "Would you like to get a copy of these?" Depending on her reply, you have options.

Let's say her response, including tone of voice and body language, translates to, "Jam it!" You say, "Jim'll have them Saturday if you change your mind." Ease out of there smoothly. You do not want other women to notice what happened. Why not? You'll see later on in a paragraph titled *Butterfly Boys Get Swatted.*

Suck it up! Maintain an outward appearance of confidence and relaxation. Do not go into the rejected, dejected mode. You know, that humiliated, tail-between-the-legs look. Your shoulders droop and your head is down as you shuffle away. That body language announces to every intuitive person in the room what just happened. By now, you do know which gender the intuitive people are, don't you?

After you recover, get back to taking pictures. When another candidate is in a shot, ask, "Would you like to get a copy of these?" She says, "Uh huh," but radiates only moderate interest with her tone of voice and other nonverbal signals.

You say, "They'll be done Wednesday," as you smile and offer your hand. When you shake, say, "Hi! I'm Don, friend of the bride." Her vibrations will let you know if you say what's just below, or if you and your twice-dinged ego move on.

Let's pretend that someone's response to your question about wanting copies is, "Sure!" as her sparkling eyes, and broad smile say, "Gee, you're kinda cute!"

What to do? Simple, just smile as you offer your hand and declare, "Hi! Don, friend of the bride." When the message she sends via her hand matches her sparkling eyes, you respond with, "Nice to meet you, Debbie. I work in Anaheim, live over in Whittier," and wait. You just hit the ball into her court.

Sometimes she doesn't notice the ball come over the net. Sometimes she's seeing if you're as brave as you are assertive so she just sits there and waits for you to show her what you're made of. Sometimes you don't notice that 235 pound boyfriend standing right behind her.

In the name of optimism, let's say her response is, "Oh yeah? I live in Fullerton." Hand her your interesting business card as you say, "Here's my number. Call me at work. I'll meet you somewhere with them on Thursday or whenever, okay?"

You have The Right Attitude, so leave for now. Go back in a half an hour. Talk with her. Dance with her. See what "develops" from those pictures. Yuk, yuk.

GETTING NOTICED–PART II

Here's another method I discovered by accident, called, "The Do You Know Him Gambit."

At any social gathering, situate yourself where you can quietly, and in confidence, say to her, "Do you know that bald guy's name? I've met him, can't remember. Don't want to embarrass myself." If she does know, or doesn't know, thank her, then move on to the bald guy. Part with, "Wish me luck." Leave now, but come back later.

I've used this to get her to notice me and as an opener after signs of interest from her. You can't lose. It's innocent looking and sounding. She feels empathy. Everyone's forgotten somebody's name.

You have a reason to move on, leaving to talk to the bald guy. And, you have the perfect excuse to talk with her again. She's wondering how it went with the bald guy, so you go back and report, right?

It works at any gathering, wet or dry. Wait awhile if people are drinking. Booze puts her at ease as it stiffens your spine.

PREVIEW OF THE RIGHT ATTITUDE

As a man, the early conversations are only to show her you're safe and interesting. Your goal in later conversations is to let her see you're an attractive, discreet man, someone it would be fun to date.

As you interact, emotional vibes and signals are exchanged. The longer you talk the better, up to a point. Five minutes into the first, and even the second conversation, it's time to move on, for a while.

To attract her you must show interest but not too much interest. Demonstrate exactly that by walking away. Later, during another conversation, the two of you can continue the courtship, if you have The Right Attitude. That's coming up shortly.

Reluctance, Resistance And Tests are imposed by women on the men who wish to court them. So, the next chapter is aimed directly at men. Even so, women can learn that some of their demands may be too much, even for Sir Gallahad.

BBC INTERVIEWS STEELE 90 minute audio tape
Bravo's Louis Theroux's Weird Weekend's producer talked with me by phone for two hours. This guy is the best interviewer on the planet! He had me explain everything I do, how I do it, why I do it, covered my years with Nathaniel Branden and everything you ever wanted to know about me! From '55 Chevies to my latest Television Shows.

Fire me up with your resistance
Put me in the mood.

BOB SEGER

Reluctance, Resistance And Tests

When I got divorced, I was so naive about court-ship and dating. The radical changes that had taken place in *The Dating Game* were shocking. Women were so distrustful, so cynical and so unwilling to take my word for anything.

I didn't realize that nowadays women do not trust any man. It took me two years to accept that it was normal for a woman to test me to see if I measured up to her standards. Does this sound familiar?

Courtship is practiced by all species in which the male is a beggar, that is, the female does not instinctively and actively seek copulation.

It should, it's from the fourth chapter! Men, the key word is *beggar*. She has what you want, but every other man wants it too. Why should she give it to you? She knows nothing about you. Your intentions and sincerity are suspect. Your manliness is unknown. Your worthiness has yet to be determined.

Before she can be persuaded, a woman must be convinced that you're worthwhile. In short, she wants to know, "Is this guy a real man, or what?"

As explained in *Courtship Tactics For Men*, coming up, few women respect, or are attracted to, men who take crap. They see it as a sign of weakness and an indication they already have you.

But, it's always necessary to show interest. However, you must maintain the *appearance* of aloofness, otherwise she'll get around to you *after* she's tested the guys who do *not* chase her.

In bars, nightclubs, spas and other pick-up situations, a woman tests you almost immediately. In other settings, she might begin testing during the first conversation but usually waits until the second or third conversation.

She starts out by pretending not to be interested. You must prove your sincere interest. If you persist, mildly but briefly, she's convinced, for the moment, at least.

A conversation or so down the road, she wants to find out if you're a real man, so she rejects you gently to see how you handle it. If you get angry, she figures she's already got you, The End. You also fail when you act like a hurt, little boy. To prove your worth, you must react like a *man*. Walk away calmly and quietly *as if* it is no big deal. Do not utter a word. The unspoken message you send is, "I was slightly interested, but no longer."

She must come to you after this happens, or you must wait for time to pass. How much? Depends. On what? How good you are at reading her body language, her mood and her real motives.

Rejecting you strongly is her way of avoiding a situation she can't handle or you came on too strong. Then again, she may think you're a jerk. It happens to us all.

Move on, but take time after your ego heals to review the entire scenario from start to crash-and-burn. Think about what you did wrong. Think about what you could have done differently. Want a guess? Before I get into that, take this side trip with me.

ASIDE ON SUBCONSCIOUS LEARNING

This is for both sexes. Want to learn from your mistakes? Want to make certain you don't commit the same errors again and again?

Immediately after you screw up, write down everything you did correctly and everything you did incorrectly. Later on when you can be truly objective, review your notes. Figure out what you wish you had done or said instead of what you did. Write that down beside the goof up.

This technique makes it easy for your subconscious to prevent future mistakes of the same kind. It now knows what you're supposed to do in that situation because you told it!

I can vouch for the unbelievable power of this technique, taught to me by my shrink and mentor, Nathaniel Branden, in 1975. It works during courtship, job interviewing, asking for a raise and all other pressure situations including dealing with difficult relatives, associates and friends. Now back to what might have gone wrong before we took this side trip.

Okay, what happened? A guess. You frightened her or offended her. A second guess. You violated *Meeting Commandment I*. Remember what it is? If not, you're doomed to get shot down again and again. For a refresher, flip back to *Commandments Of Meeting*.

PRESSURE OR PERSISTENCE

Directing and controlling her desire to be persuaded by you is an ever-present fear of the consequences. At the same time, she loves the excitement of the moment. If you don't offend her or scare her away, she wants more. But, it must be at the pace she's capable of enjoying.

If she feels pressure to move faster, she will dig in her heels, figuratively, and resist. Once this happens, you will get nowhere by trying to persuade her. Back off! Be patient not persistent. Wait until you "accidentally" cross her path again.

Make *Meeting Commandment I* your touchstone. If you startle her, radiate lust or even momentarily embarrass her during the crucial opening moments, all is lost. Make only a friendly, relaxed gesture. Smile and say, "Hi." Resist the urge to take charge.

Don't get me wrong. There are times when she'll be most excited and interested by your direct, strong approach. However, you will make few, if any, fatal mistakes by waiting to see if coming on hard is what's really needed.

PATIENCE PREVENTS GAMES

To avoid the dangers of emotional and sexual intimacy, insecure and immature females, of all ages, play *Rapo*. And, inadequate men play *Cavalier*.

When you come on strong and you're impatient, you become the perfect victim for her, or his, little game. Take your time. Have another sip of champagne. Ask yourself, "Too smooth? Too willing? Too good to be true?" Have another sip and mull over the answers you come up with.

Remember, identify a *Rapo* or *Cavalier* player by how calm and relaxed they are during their interaction with you. They're not nervous. It's only a game.

Women, if you have not read the *Preface,* please do so now, before you read the blunt talk in the next chapter, *Courtship Tactics For Women.*

All men only want one thing!

MOM AND DAD

Courtship Tactics For Women

Many women do not realize how much power they have, especially during the early stages of courtship. I believe many women make poor choices in men because they do not feel powerful. They think they have to make do with any guy they can get. To feel powerful, you must know *why* you are powerful, then accept, in your guts, that you *are* powerful.

PLATITUDE REVISION TIME

Let's re-phrase what Mom and Dad told you about men so that you have a more realistic view of the world and a more powerful regard for yourself. Instead of, their well meant, *All men only want one thing!* Shift it to, *You have what he wants.*

Understand that once he is interested in you, *he* is the beggar. You are the powerful one. Why are you powerful? because you can say "no," at any time. In every human relationship, from love to employment, the person who says "no," has all the power.

DEFINE YOUR TASKS

Let's define exactly what you must accomplish. In short, you must: Find him. Attract him. Meet and talk with him. Get him interested enough to date you.

84 BODY LANGUAGE SECRETS

FIND HIM

Let's be honest. The man you want to meet, Mr. Right, is not desperate. He is not searching. He is taking care of himself. Don't you agree? If so, please accept that Mr. Right is *not* looking for you or anybody else. He's busy with his life and his interests.

Do *not* try to find him any place where men try to meet women. Why not? (1) Most men who hang out in bars or clubs are losers with no life. (2) Women who frequent those places are hardened meat-market pros. Why compete with pros? (3) Even if he is there, his guard is up to protect himself from manipulative, game-playing liars. When his guard is up, you can't tell if he is Mr. Right or Mr. Hyde.

Find him when he's *not* looking for women. You will *catch* him, pun intended, with his guard down. Where? Parties at friends or acquaintances; wedding receptions; playing sports you play such as volleyball or softball; taking classes like Swiss Franc Investing, Auto Mechanics or Stock Market Fundamentals; attending a club meeting such as Chamber of Commerce, Rotary, Elks, or Lions.

Besides bars, other places that are packed with losers: how to meet people seminars, pop psychology workshops of any kind, and all gatherings sponsored by singles clubs.

ATTRACT HIM

The woman who brazenly exhibits her physical assets will get the attention of every man in the room, initially. However, after a short time, most men lose interest. She has revealed everything. There is no untold story. There is no mystery. There is no reason to start, let alone, continue the chase.

Exceptions are adolescent boys of all ages and men who want an arm-charm or those seeking an attractive physical presence, not a real woman.

SECRETS ATTRACT MEN

Men love secrets. They join secret clubs with secret signs and secret passwords. They love spy novels and movies about manly men who steal secrets. To strongly attract, then hold a man's attention, and interest, you must have a secret.

ATTIRE SECRETS

Half of the story is more engaging than the whole story. A backless dress with an inherently modest front is a strong draw once he sees you from the rear. Long skirts with moderately suggestive splits are far more enticing than short shirts.

The hope of catching a glimpse of your breast down that slightly scooped neckline is far more arousing than cleavage. We hang around hoping you will lean over further next time.

Tight jeans, tight skirts, and tight tops are attention grabbers. But, they reveal, rather than appetizingly conceal, thus only attract the immature or lascivious. Why stick around after we've seen everything you've got?

Anticipation is arousing. Be secretive. Be suggestive. Be almost-but-not-quite. Lure us with the unknown. Imply there's much more than meets our eye.

FIRST, CATCH HIS EYE

Waiting for Mr. Right or Prince Charming to notice you is futile unless you are as beautiful, as built and as well dressed as Cinderella.

Bend over and fix your shoe. Any and all movement attracts attention. But this particular move also exposes your bottom—a primal attention grabber.

Walk across the room, then begin a striptease by peeling off your blazer and hanging it on a chair.

Create more movement. Visit the rest room. During the trip, you conduct an ancient courtship ritual, the promenade. All the males notice, then check you out, somewhat discreetly, as you pass by.

If he's sitting behind you, reach back, lift your hair and fluff it in a pretense at increasing your comfort. This exposes your *secret* bare neck. Be brief, only a glimpse to peak his interest.

If standing with your back to him, put your hands in the rear pockets of your jeans or slacks. The movement draws his eyes to you, then to your buttocks. Once again, primal, thus difficult to ignore.

SECOND, CALL HIM OVER

You are doubly powerful. You have the power to attract him and at the same time, the power to reassure him.

Eye contact followed by a smile is the most effective attention getter any woman has. It costs nothing. It is safe. It is simple. Do it!

When you look at a man and smile, you nonverbally say, *"Hi! How ya doin'. I'm friendly. I don't bite."* Now that's a message every man loves.

Doubt me? Think about how you react when anyone, man, woman or child smiles at you. That's exactly how we men feel when you smile at us.

Remember, a man must be reassured that you are not going to embarrass him by laughing at him or rejecting him rudely if he comes over to chat with you. The smile you send is your first act of reassurance.

FURTHER ATTENTION REQUIRED

Some men need to be reassured more than once. Some of us are shy no matter how much bravado we exude. A few of us have been hurt in the past and aren't certain that someone who merely smiled is actually interested. Then there are those of us who aren't not that socially adept, thus we don't get the first message you send.

Don't give up if your first smile doesn't have the

impact you want. Wait a few minutes, then give him a louder, stronger signal.

Without looking at him, gradually shift your posture to erect then turn so your body is facing him. Pull your shoulders back slightly to make your breasts more prominent. Now, look directly at him. Continue to stare until he looks at you. When he does, hold his eyes for longer than socially appropriate, then smile briefly and look down in a slightly submissive way to break off eye contact.

WHEN HE COMES OVER

After the awkward, exciting first few moments have passed, if he does not offer his name and shake hands, offer your hand and your name. Use the immense power of touch to communicate whatever you want him to know about you. At the same time use your intuition to learn as much about him as you can during those precious few seconds.

KEEP HIM INTERESTED

Most men love to talk about themselves. After the standard obligatory questions and statements, always ask him something about himself that gets him talking. Typical subjects men can ramble on forever about and enjoy themselves, thus you:

Athletic deeds	Gambling wins
College shenanigans	Ideas to make money.
Manly hobbies	Military service exploits
His first car	Present job, dream job
Foreign travel	Favorite movies

At the beginning of his monologue, encourage him by *appearing* to listen attentively as follows: lean forward, nod, give him a few "uh huh's," raise your eyebrows, tilt your head. Keep your hands off your face and mouth. Don't cross your arms in front of your chest. Don't steeple.

After he gets into to it, use your intuition to determine if you like him or not. Send him the signals that match your decision.

ESSENCE OF ATTRACTING MEN

As a woman you have the power to send discreet and distinct, yet potent, signals without words, thus without risk. Once again, use what you have.

Beyond smiling at him from across the room, the most powerful thing you can do is touch him. After shaking his hand, touch him. It makes no difference when, how, where or why. Two or three times during the first conversation is an excellent start.

Brush his hand lightly when handing him something. Admire and touch any of his accessories or attire. "Accidentally" bump his leg with your knee as you change positions. Any semi-plausible reason or accident or excuse is fine.

Much of the next chapter, *Courtship Tactics For Men,* applies to women as well. The parts that don't are obvious.

ARTS & ENTERTAINMENT SHOW, *Seminar, Interviews Video!*
A&E crew came to Whittier and taped us for ten hours for LOVE CONNECTION a national hour-long show on Older-Younger. The best part is a mini seminar Joanna and I conducted. We prepared three guys to attend an art exhibit and reception at a local gallery. The young women, provided by A&E. During rehearsal and the real, on-camera seminar, Joanna covered shoes, slacks, shirts, sideburns, hair cuts/styles, unbuttoning shirts and shirt sleeves, teeth, sunglasses, shorts, tank tops, colors for shirts and on and on. I covered What Do You Have That She Wants, body language basics.

Nobody wants to be second fiddle.

THE AUTHOR'S MOTHER
About taking a stand on who I should ask to the prom.

Courtship Tactics For Men

All my life I've heard that love comes along when you least expect it. I can vouch for the truth of that adage except for the very first time.

I was *trying* to meet someone when I met my first wife. I was 19, she was 17. My friend and I were cruising the boulevard. She and her friend were promenading.

Twelve years later, my second wife walked into my life when I least expected it. Later, in June of 1993, I went to a local coffee shop simply to escape my sweltering house and met Joanna. We live in paradise, on the Big Island of Hawaii. This book is dedicated to her.

Here's more evidence. Since divorcing in 1982, I have never been able to date a woman I met in some other way than being introduced by a mutual friend or she introduced herself or I introduced myself at: (a) social gathering (b) class or club meeting (c) my company or (d) her work place after being a customer for weeks.

Okay men! What conclusion can we reach from these facts? When you're *not* trying, you have The Right Attitude.

THE RIGHT ATTITUDE DEFINED

As explained in *Reluctance, Resistance And Tests,* when you are obvious about being strongly interested, some women write you off as a pushover. With others, if you radiate too much indifference, it causes them to lose face. The End. Finally, other women believe that just by being friendly, *they* are chasing *you!* So what works?

Nearly all women are attracted to a man who won't kiss ass. They are strongly drawn by self-confidence, feigned or real.

In short, she will date you, if you're friendly but slightly aloof, relaxed but powerful and confident without being arrogant. Your *unspoken* attitude must be:

> *I'm not going to chase you. Sure, I'm friendly, but I'm friendly with everyone. Yeah, I'm somewhat interested. It might be possible if you, lady, play your cards right. Well, gotta go. Catch you later. By the way, you're not bad.*

Here's how you communicate The Right Attitude without words.

SLIGHTLY ALOOF	HIGHLY INTERESTED
Sometimes open posture	All openness
Body usually angled away	Body facing her
Rarely lean toward her	Always lean toward her
Neutral or pleasant face	Moderately serious
Preen now and again	Preen often
Relaxed posture	Erect, ready posture
Rarely touch her	Touch as often as possible
Polite smiles	Broad smiles
Occasional, intense eye contact	Look her in the eyes
Caress yourself once	Caress yourself regularly
Hold your glass steady	Finger glass sensually

As you talk, make her feel like she must try harder before you'll make a move. The best course to follow is showing brief flashes of intense sexual and romantic interest. Not with words, right? Separate these with long periods of being pleasant while remaining moderately aloof.

DOMINANCE AND SUBMISSION

Once in a while throw in a few digs and a bit of sarcasm to irritate her. This keeps her off balance and guessing about you. It also makes it clear that she must fish or cut bait as well as forcing her to realize that she will get nowhere is she's only just engaging in, what she considers, harmless flirting.

During it all you must nonverbally demonstrate that you are dominant. The simplest act of aggression is to lean into her personal space briefly, then lean back out, as you continue talking all the while. Use any pretense, such as setting your glass on the coffee table.

Another way to dominate is to briefly become larger than she is. When you are both sitting, stand up as if you're getting the kinks out, but keep talking as you tower over her, then sit back down.

After demonstrating that you are the dominant one, you must reassure her that you intend no harm. If you stood up to tower over her, after you sit down, adopt a timid, shy posture for a couple of seconds. If you leaned into her personal space, do the same when you lean back out.

APPEARANCES COUNT

Confident people are not in a hurry, not pushy, not nervous or excited. Moving slowly and talking slowly at least *gives the appearance* of confidence. First impressions are lasting impressions.

Take your time. Don't be too happy, too excited or too interested. Of course, this applies to women as well as men and not just in courtship settings, but also in business and office politics.

DON'T ACT SUPERIOR

During all conversations, don't act like a parent or professor. If she asks for advice like she'd ask a good friend, carefully say what you think. Be certain you are talking with her as an equal. If she indirectly asks for advice, beg off or play dumb. Coming across as better than she is always wrong.

SIGNS OF SUPERIORITY AND ARROGANCE

Steepling	Hands on back of head
Looking down one's nose	Examines one's cuticles
Nose in the air	Arms crossed on chest
Peering over one's glasses	Patronizing compliments
Hands behind back	Fatherly pats
Feet on anything	Snorting through nose

STEEPLING

With palms facing, the person's fingertips become the top of a church steeple. From there, he, or she, pontificates. Readily seen on talk shows as the guest enlightens us all. Low steepling and disguised steepling are similar but usually indicate confidence rather than superiority.

LOOKING DOWN ONE'S NOSE

Proclaims, *I am above you.* Commonly adopted by insecure bosses. Also prevalent among full-of-himself types who have developed large but false egos in a futile attempt at having some self-esteem.

NOSE IN THE AIR

Insinuates, *Somebody around here stinks and it's not me.* Also, as with looking down one's nose, proclaims, *I am above you.* Common among insecure blue bloods and wannabe blue bloods.

HANDS BEHIND BACK

The person (king) is so confident that no one would *dare* harm him that he stands and walks in a blatantly vulnerable manner. British Bobbies often adopt this posture, as do corporate types who see themselves as royalty.

DISGUISED HIGH STEEPLING *means the person is confident but arrogant. He knows more than the people he's talking with. In this photo, the person is also touching his mouth. That means he is also preventing himself from saying something. The sentence he's not saying is, "You poor things. You know absolutely nothing."*

HIGH STEEPLING *combined with looking down one's nose. Disgusting but revealing. It means he has a holier-than-thou attitude. It's a posture often assumed by corporate royalty and politicians who consider themselves the equal of Popes and Kings or Queens.*

MODERATE HIGH STEEPLING *Means she's certain that she knows what she's talking about or, if listening, confident she knows more than the speaker. High steepling also puts barrier between the person and the audience to whom he, or she is preaching.*

LOW STEEPLING *Means he is confident that he knows what he's talking about. When compared with all the other forms of steepling, it's only mildly offensive.*

TOUCHING *YOUR* PROPERTY Attempts to intimidate and communicate without words, *I am so superior to you that I can take your property. I do not have to show you any respect.* Even if it is your desk, when he puts his hand or foot on it, the desk becomes his possession, literally.

HANDS BEHIND HEAD OR NECK Attempts to intimidate by communicating, "I am so superior to you that I can be lackadaisical toward you. I don't have to show you any respect."

PEERING OVER ONE'S GLASSES Taking a second look to imply, "You can't possibly mean that, fool!" Attempts to intimidate without words.

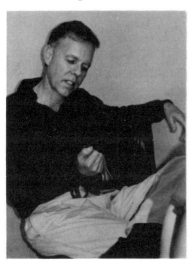

EXAMINES CUTICLES *During conversation, the arrogant person inspects his cuticles or finger tips instead of making eye contact with the other person. Usually done while listening. Implies, "My finger nails are far more important than paying attention to you."*

ARMS CROSSED ON CHEST *The arrogant person says, in effect, "I am so superior to you that I am completely closed to you and your ideas. Say anything you want. I am not going to listen."*

BE AN EQUAL BUT POWERFUL

Explain anything like it's simple and only a matter of looking it up. You just happen to know this because you read about it or do it for a living or whatever. She, or he, could have known it, too.

Tactfully done, talking about something she's asked about or wants to learn about is dynamite. It clearly shows how much better off she'd be dating you. The way you want her to come away from a conversation is "Gee, he's the kinda guy I'd like go out with, learn how to scuba dive." As opposed to, "Wow! is he smart."

OVERALL ADVICE

Men, the most dangerous enemy you face is from within. Your lack of confidence; your too confident, too aggressive manner; or your lack of aggression.

These are tough to overcome, even with practice, so the best general strategy is to be unpredictable, swinging between being nice and being indifferent. It keeps her off balance and enables you to maintain an effective perspective on the relationship. Without the right viewpoint, you are liable to be wrapped around her finger in a couple of days.

I must stress this once again. With women of any age, when you're obvious or up front about wanting to go out with her, there's no longer a challenge or the excitement of not knowing if you'll make a move or not. So, when she's certain about your interest, she convinces herself the outcome is so obvious she doesn't have to take a chance and make even a safe date, like just having coffee. It's not *Rapo*, but the result is the same.

Pay attention to the signals she's sending you. You'll know what's going on most of the time. But, if it feels like she's coming on to you, even when there's nothing concrete you can point to as evidence, she is. That's what courtship is all about.

When talking and interacting with her don't make sexual comments. Don't talk about how great you are. Let manners and etiquette show. Don't try to impress her. All other guys try that. She often deciphers the attempt as, "He wants me. I've got him."

At the same time, let her see you have attributes and knowledge she'll benefit from in the near future. When it fits, always mention some of the things you like to do that are different from most men—attend plays, go the thoroughbred races or drive to Beverly Hills for Sunday brunch at an elegant restaurant.

Once more, Don't with a capital D, say or do any of these things to impress her. If she even slightly suspects you're trying, it ruins everything because it makes her think she's already got you.

BUTTERFLY BOYS GET SWATTED

A butterfly flits from flower to flower drinking the nectar. The guy who hits on one woman and then another soon gets shot down.

Bide your time. Evaluate all the data coming at you. Do NOT go talk to the first or even the second woman who smiles at you. Smile and nod. Make a mental note. Keep your smile friendly and non-committal. Circulate. Send out your signals. Notice the signals women are sending you.

> *Mo' betta go easy, mo' betta go slow.*
> HAWAIIAN PHILOSOPHY

The woman who sees herself as your second choice is not interested. She wants to be number one, just as we all do. Nobody wants to be second fiddle.

ESSENCE OF THE RIGHT ATTITUDE

During courtship, and later when you're dating, she must know with her entire being, that you will walk away forever if she insists on behaving badly. Your firm commitment to this act of self-respect cannot be faked. It must be genuine, heartfelt and be an integral part of your overall personality.

Body Language Anecdote From the World Of Office Politics I was a quick-learning 32 when I made it to the top floor of the corporation. The guys up here were battle-hardened veterans. They had prevailed in the never-ending struggle for position, prestige and power that dominates corporate life. The name of the game was, and is, Intimidate To Dominate. The only rule was, There Are No Rules.

Harvey Brush, Senior Executive Vice President, was sent to LA from corporate headquarters to "straighten out that _bleeping_ mess." On Harvey's second day, as I was sitting in my boss' office reviewing the problems with our billion dollar proposal effort. Harvey barged in, put his size 14 wing-tip on the edge of Maury's polished ebony desk, grunted as he bent over to tie his shoe he let fly an outrageously loud fart. He smirked, looked right at Maury and said, "Somebody stepped on a frog, har, har, har!"

I was stunned into immobility. My boss managed a small smile as he waited quietly to be addressed.

Without removing his foot, "How's it goin' on the proposal guys? We really need that bastard!" Harvey bellowed as he looked from my boss to me and back.

I don't remember what Maury or I managed to mumble. But I still remember that there was no doubt in anyone's mind who was in charge. And, there was no doubt in my mind that the proposal would be the best one I had ever managed.

FINAL WARNING

Some women are blatant in their come ons. There is no mistaking what's happening. Be suspicious if she's relaxed and smooth. Even when it seems like she's really inviting you to make your move, it may be nothing more than bait so she can rebuff your proposition and win the little game of *Rapo* she's playing.

If you're talking about a subject that is inappropriate, persuasion becomes impossible. *What To Talk About,* the next chapter, keeps you on track.

What to leave out, what to leave in.

BOB SEGAR, *Against The Wind*

What To Talk About

The essence of early courtship conversations is to communicate, with and without words, *This is who I am. I like myself. I hope you like me. Tell me about yourself so I can discover if I like you.*

DYNAMICS—A MAN'S PERSPECTIVE

In the game of backgammon, opening moves are so crucial the outcome is often decided in 30 seconds. It's the same in this game. When you do and say the right things during the critical first moments, the moments turn into minutes. The longer you sustain contact, the easier it is for her to see you're *safe*, then *interesting*. Only after that, can she find you *attractive*.

Once she's decided you're not a threat, she discreetly checks you out physically as the conversation continues. If you measure up, and if you don't break any of the *Eleven Commandments of Meeting*, two things take place during the next few minutes. First, she decides if you're a playboy. If you do nothing and say nothing that makes her think you are one, the next thing she does is wonder what you'd be like, should you persuade her.

To persuade her, you must reveal yourself so she can decide. Talk about what you like and dislike as you give her plenty of openings to do the same thing.

STANDARD CONVERSATION

The typical courtship conversation is a casual chat at a wedding reception. The first topic is how you and she know the newly married couple. You go first and tell her. "Hi. I'm Don, on Sally's volleyball team."

If she doesn't reciprocate, help her past these awkward first few moments. Give her something she can handle easily, no matter how anxious she may be. Something like, "Do you know Sally from college?"

It makes no difference what she says, you should always respond with information about yourself. "Oh yeah? I've known Sally for three years, met her when I joined the team with Roger, over there, my boss at Hawaiian Antiques. Do you play volleyball?"

The key is giving her information about you, so she'll give you information about herself, then you'll have something to talk about.

You can always say, "Nice reception, great band." Or, "Nice weather we're having." It's safe, not helpful. These statements are useful when your brain freezes, as it will from time to time.

You have to defrost it quickly though and get back to revealing yourself. "Seen that new talk show with Danny Bonaduce? It's like the others but I keep asking myself when the rest of the Partridge Family's going to come on. Weird!"

For example, "Did you like the Partridge Family?" Or, "Sally and Allan always come to my annual Raider Party. She doesn't like football but loves to party. You like pro football?"

Always, reveal yourself first, then give her the

chance to do likewise, "You know Sally from college?" "You play volleyball?"

Only show your interest nonverbally so she can respond nonverbally, that way no one's afraid of being rejected. Send her a few subtle signals of interest as you keep your eyes open for her signals.

SAFE SUBJECTS ONLY

Your views on capital punishment have nothing to do with the emotional and physical attraction of courtship. Reveal yourself while talking about movies, television shows, music, colleges, skiing, back packing, cars, sport teams, beach weather, where you've been recently, or are about to go.

FORBIDDEN TOPICS

Never discuss religion. Avoid emotion-producing subjects: abortion, civil rights, welfare, sex, politics, well, you get the idea.

Sex is verboten during early conversations. Don't bring up the subject in any fashion. Don't respond in kind to her sexual innuendoes or off color jokes. Change the subject without making her feel as if she committed a *faux pas*. Don't swear even if she says "fuck" every few sentences. Some women do much of this as a test to see if you're interested in her as a sex toy or if you like her as a person. Pass the test.

MEN'S VIEW OF WOMEN AND PROFANITY

Most men are disoriented by a female who swears a lot or they think she's an easy lay. As a woman, reserve profanity for moments when you need to be emphatic. Save vulgarities for crucial situations when you want his undivided attention so you can make a key point.

MEN MUST ALWAYS SAY

During each conversation, genuinely compliment her *once*, and only *once*. Your compliment must be genuine because most women are able to identify bullshit at 1000 yards.

As stressed previously, comment on something that others don't normally notice. Not her beautiful hair. Not her beautiful eyes. Not her beautiful complexion. Maybe her teeth. But, if you can notice something that reveals her personal taste, she knows you're different, and special. Her clothes, shoes, jewelry and accessories are the ways she makes a statement about herself.

WOMEN MUST ALWAYS SAY

During each conversation, compliment him on something you genuinely like. However, if you are not used to complimenting men, it is a skill that can be readily learned. The key is to be observant. Look him over, head to toe. Find something you sincerely like. Then tell him that you do, in a matter of fact manner.

MEN MUST NEVER SAY

Absolutely never say, "I'm never getting married again." Never volunteer that you're dating other women. Don't belittle her beliefs, values or tastes. Keep your cynicism to yourself. Don't mention or look at another female. Don't knock marriage and children.

SECOND CONVERSATIONS

When you can weave it in without being obvious, disclose yourself as single and available, "When I got divorced, bla bla." Or, "My ex-girl friend used to, bla bla."

Statements about yourself are best, followed by a question. But ask questions carefully. Don't seem nosy or trying to find out where she lives. You're a suspected molester. She doesn't want you following her home, at least not yet. More about this delicate topic in a few paragraphs.

Talk about anything she's interested in. Keep the

topics non-controversial but show yourself. Give her plenty of opportunities to reciprocate. That's what this phase is all about.

Reveal more of yourself in second and third conversations. What kind of music, cars, clothes, food, restaurants, and such you like. Later, or, even now, if the time is right, reveal what you like to do that's radically different.

Talking about places you've been or are going is always good unless you come across as trying to impress her. If you're able to discuss it without trying to dazzle her, travel is a good, safe, useful topic.

As always, you go first to find out if she's geographically desirable, too. Delicately weave in where you live and which town you work in. You're putting the ball in her court. If she gives you this info, it's solid evidence she's attracted to you, even if done in an oh-by-the-way manner.

Don't push this. Right now it's not important, so don't blow it. If she reciprocates, great. If not, wait a few sentences or paragraphs. Don't put any pressure on. It can be done with grace and subtleness, "Is that a long drive from where you live?" after she mentions where she goes to school or works or plays. If that doesn't get it out of her, wait a while, then say, "So which town do you live in?" but only when the time is right. "Where do you live?" is direct and makes her stumble, as well as feeling pressure. "You from around here?" is a bush league, boy's move, demonstrating strong interest too soon.

Keep talking. Keep revealing yourself. Listen for anything she says that makes it feasible to suggest future contact for any reason.

SETTING IT UP TO DATE HER

The set up includes disclosing you're single and available as described above. Other setups include thinking of some way she could do you a favor. Like asking if she knows anyone with a VW Thing for sale or if she sees one for sale to tell you. Anything to get her to think about you when you're not there.

What can you do a woman usually can't? Hook up car stereos and home stereos, video cassette recorders and other mysterious electronic devices? Can you do income tax returns? Think. Make a list of what you can do *before* you meet her.

LATER CONVERSATIONS AND BEYOND

Continue revealing yourself, especially things you like to do that she's probably never tried. Other than that, you only have to talk about topics of interest to her.

Today, before you meet her, sit down and write a slanted, interesting one page autobiography. Commit it to memory. She'll ask, probably after two conversations, about you and your history. On the first real date, she'll want to know details, somewhat like a pedigree. Don't brag. Do say what you've accomplished that you're proud of.

Be ready to discuss your divorce honestly and without sadness or regret in your eyes, tone of voice or on your face. If you can't do this, you're not ready for her no matter how ready you are in all other ways.

Don't be afraid to say you've screwed up. It makes you a human being. Don't dwell on it and come across like a loser or a basket case.

At this point, with and without words, you have passed her tests and proven that you are potentially worthy.

My advice about not *asking* for a date, but rather, *suggesting* a date, is covered in *Dating,* the next chapter, and the next step of this courtship.

I don't care where we go
I don't care what we do
I don't care pretty baby
just take me with you.
PRINCE

Let's spend the night together.
MICK JAGGER

Dating

What is a date? The next to last step of courtship. It's any activity undertaken in the pretext of having fun so that the female has time to decide, consciously or subconsciously, if she has been persuaded by a worthy male.

Men, it took persistence, time and patience to interest her and prove yourself. Even now that she's attracted, more of the same is required for her to be persuaded to take the last step. Don't remember what the last step is? Flip back to *What Is Courtship* and refresh your memory as to why we human animals go through this elaborate courtship business.

FIRST DATES

The purpose of a first date is to show her that you really are worthy. You only need a few hours.

Use your head. What has she mentioned during conversation? Suggesting a drink is fine. It's not much to ask for, it's got a built-in time limit, thus easy to accept.

Lunch at the park is on neutral turf. There, you're both equally distant from home base. No one is too defensive. But it's more of a commitment unless you add, "I've got to be back by 2 PM."

Sunday brunch is great. During the suggestion make it easier to accept by time limiting it. Add that you have to be somewhere by 3 PM.

A dinner date is too much for starters. In our culture it implies dinner *and*. Save it for later on after things have heated up.

DON'T ASK

Want to ruin everything? Just say one of these: "Would you like to," "If you're not busy," "Can you."

Why? Because The Right Attitude that attracts and fascinates her turns to wispy smoke the instant you ask for permission.

Suggest, don't ask. "I like talking with you. Let's have brunch Sunday, at Charlie Brown's." Make statements. Be positive. You're in charge here.

Maintain The Right Attitude. You'd like to date her but you're not dying to. It would be cool, but if she says "no," it's not even a slight ripple in your world. You're relaxed. You know she wants to go out with you, will go out with you, if you proposition her the right way, next week or next month.

THE SUPREMACY OF TOUCH

Touch is the most powerful, most reliable sense we have. When we doubt our eyes as to whether or not the flowers on the restaurant table are real, we reach out and touch them.

With their differently wired brains, women have the ability to discern even the most subtle meaning in a man's touch. As a woman, use this ability to assure yourself that he is what you think he is, even when this stage has been reached.

On Shaking Hands explained that as a woman, you have the ability to communicate a tremendous amount of information about yourself, your motives, your wants, your needs, your dislikes as well as your limits, simply by the way you touch a man. Use what you have.

IT ALWAYS BEGINS WITH A TOUCH

We were raised in a culture where touching is generally unacceptable. If you doubt this, notice how we behave in an elevator!

The point is, during the early stages of a date, the two of you must get used to touching each other, but it must be done gradually.

In the unwritten courtship rules of our society, it is not proper for a man to touch a woman for at least ten minutes. Then, his touch must be socially appropriate so that his real purpose is disguised. For example, he can ask to see her heirloom ring, then gently touch her hand, ever so briefly, as he admires the ring and talks with her about it's age and origin.

But, the same unwritten rules say it's okay for the woman to touch the man almost immediately, however, she must also be socially appropriate so that her real purpose is disguised. For example, a woman can put her hand on a man's hand or wrist under the pretext of getting his attention or she can reach out and feel his tie if she says at the same time, "Nice! Quite different."

Caution! Men, if you try *too* hard not to touch her because you don't want to appear inappropriate, she may feel unattractive and rejected on a subconscious, possibly even a conscious, level.

TOUCH AS OFTEN AS POSSIBLE

Women, if you like him and the way things are proceeding, touch him early and often. Then as things continue, you can increase or decrease the pace and intensity of the arousal simply by touching him or withholding your touch.

Men, she must get used to the feel of you. Touch her at every socially acceptable opportunity from the first moment. Each time you touch her, she is able to subconsciously judge your worthiness and attractiveness.

Help with her sweater, admire her bracelet or necklace. (Careful Buddy!) Pat her on the back for a great joke or other excuse. Help her put on, or take off her coat, take her arm as you open the car door and gently guide her, "accidentally" brush her hand as you give her the menu. Don't be obviously trying to touch her! That puts you in the Dirty Old Man category instantly.

EBB AND FLOW

A successful date (she is being persuaded) has a rhythm to it. Anticipation, excitement and arousal come and go. They intermingle with pleasant relaxation and enjoyable conversation, which, in turn, are replaced by anticipation and arousal.

EXCHANGE SIGNALS

When the pace is correct, the signals that both people send are ever-increasing interest, readiness and excitement. As she is more fully persuaded, the woman gradually grows more submissive and the man gradually becomes more dominate.

From the woman's point of view, she must be prepared to signal the man to slow down if he's coming on too strong. At the same time, if he's persuading her, she must project arousal and excitement mixed with coy resistance.

From the man's point of view, he must nonverbally project confidence, power and dominance except when reassuring her. As always, he must maintain The Right Attitude.

Remember, this is a situation in which your ego can get destroyed in less than a heartbeat. You can be humiliated for weeks by a few choice words or even a look. Thus, during it all, both man and woman need to interweave signs of reassurance.

WHAT TO WATCH OUT FOR

The key nonverbal signals a man must be on

guard for are signs of nervousness or anxiety. When he notices any, he must slow down and reassure her.

He must also be prepared to notice boredom, impatience or anger and make appropriate adjustments. Sometimes he must ask her directly to determine if it's the activity that is causing the problem, such as playing video games in an arcade when she would prefer just walking along the avenue and window shopping.

The topic of conversation may be boring, or she may be restless with the slow service at the restaurant. Then again, he may be dominating the conversation by regaling her with tales of his grand exploits.

SIGNS OF BOREDOM

Looking at wristwatch	Doodling
Asking what time it is	Drumming fingertips
Tapping foot	Swinging leg
Blank stare	Head in hand
Drooped eyelids	Hand on side of face or head

SUSTAINED VERBAL INTERCOURSE

Men and women, keep the conversation light and pleasant. Avoid controversial subjects. Reveal your likes and dislikes in movies, sports, food, travel, drinks, games, and such. Arranging a second date is much easier after finding out where you two fit together. Work into the conversation things you like to do and places you like to go.

Men, when she reciprocates, ask some questions, then add, "That sounds like it might be fun. Let's go there *sometime*," and see what her reaction is. Don't firm it up even when she's very positive. Wait.

If she knows how to do something that you don't, see if she'd like to teach you, *sometime*. If she knows of an interesting restaurant, again say, "It might be fun to go there *sometime*."

SET UP A SECOND DATE

Men, if she asks you with a time and day, fine, she's serious. Go ahead and make a date. But when she asks casually, she may be testing. So, say, "That sounds like fun. Let me check my schedule. I'll call you."

Don't appear to have an open calendar or to be willing to shift things around to fit her offer. You're a man, a busy powerful man. Don't accommodate your life to anyone's schedule. You're the catch here. You have The Right Attitude.

Want to ruin everything? Say or suggest or imply: "When can we get together again?" or, "When will I see you again?" or "Let's do this again sometime soon." Why? Because you're chasing her, and that destroys the attraction of The Right Attitude.

Do let her know in plain English you are having fun talking with, and being with her. But don't *ask* for a second date.

A SECOND DATE, MAYBE

For her to want a second date with you, the first date has to be a great experience. Have fun together. You want her to think, *That was great. He's fun. Wonder why he didn't even try to kiss me good night? Maybe he doesn't like me.*

Men, even if something's been semi-setup, wait a few days, then call and talk for a while. See how the vibrations are. If they're positive, *suggest,* don't ask for, a non-romantic date. If she's negative, sit back and wait for her to call you. It'll be a long wait, like the rest of your life.

However, when she's neutral, don't ask, *suggest* a non-romantic date. When she declines with a realistic-sounding excuse, wait a week or more then try once more. If she still has an excuse, see above regarding what to do when she's negative.

Men, after the first date, if she doesn't want to go out with you again, she won't no matter what you propose. Don't chase. You have The Right Attitude.

PERSUASION IN ACTION

Each of us has seen the supreme climax of courtship. We all share the knowledge of perfection. Rhett stops talking, sweeps Scarlett off her feet and climbs the stairs with her in his arms.

Men, that can be you, if you follow the advice in the next chapter.

To many women, and some men, the next chapter is shocking as well as depressing. It is aimed at divorced men who were married for a substantial amount of time, thus do not understand the realities that single women face at the beginning of the 21st Century.

However, many women who reviewed early versions of the book appreciated the chapter. The gist of their comments was, "Yeah, I don't like it, but I can see some of that in myself. Especially about wanting him to prove it by changing to nice."

Everyone, please persist during, *On Not Being Too Nice.*

THE POWER SUIT a A POWERFUL VIDEO!
The most important principle of Steel Balls is: First you have to look like somebody she wants to talk with. *[Translation: Somebody she wants to talk with.]* THE POWER SUIT makes an Impact on her, not an impression! Don Steele shows you secret details of selecting, getting it tailored perfectly, and wearing **The Power Suit.** Includes exclusive footage from Don's Suit Shopping Tours and his TRA workshops. ETA late 2003 or early 2004.

Treat me mean, treat me cruel
but love me.

ELVIS

On Not Being Too Nice

Men, not being too nice is a mandatory, all inclusive mandate you must follow to have The Right Attitude.

Of course she wants you to treat her nicely, fairly and with respect. However, what you consider nice, fair and respectful is rarely what she hopes for. Why? Because every woman is an individual human being with her own story to tell, her own personal goals, values and morals, just like you.

She has a unique history of bad and good times at the hand of males, beginning with Daddy, followed by boyfriends, fiancées, and ex-husbands. Many have also had an ego-crushing, heart-breaking experience with a master manipulator like the professional game player, Randy RedPorsche.

> Women, if this information does not apply to you, ignore it. **Caution!** If it does apply, don't take it personally. I'm merely reporting a well-known, documented phenomenon. However, if it does apply, a heart-felt re-examination of your values and expectations is in order.

I love being nice. It is my nature to be nice to anyone I like but even more so to women I enjoy. By *nice* I mean considerate, polite, open, vulnerable, giving, attentive, appreciative, warm, accepting, gentle, demonstrative and expressive with my affection, and such.

During the early aftermath of my divorce I found women to be unappreciative, even offended by my inclination to be nice. I was shocked and disappointed.

I soon learned that nearly all women find this behavior unacceptable in any male. There have been a couple of wonderful exceptions but even those women resisted being treated well at first.

Meeting someone nice disorients her. I don't know if she thinks it's too good to be true. I do know many women saw me as a wimp and lost respect, as well as interest, quickly. How do I know? Because I got tired of striking out and asked in simple English, "What did I do wrong?" Good old feedback.

Here are some possibilities. She's been treated poorly for so long by Daddy, her boyfriends and her ex-husband that it seems normal, manly. Or, she's been catered to for so long she's tired of it. Daddy spoiled her. Jimmy adored her. Her ex chases her. She wants you to "act like a man." Then again, she may be like many people who perceive *nice* as weak.

A WOMAN'S VIEW ON 'NICE'

This letter is by 22 year old Hillary Heinz, Eugene, Oregon, in response to an advice columnist asking why women put up with abysmal treatment from boyfriends.

Although I swore I would never put myself through the torture I saw several friends go through, I broke up with several wonderful (nice) guys to obsess over an unattainable jerk. Then I clung to a guy who was nicer to strangers at the bus stop than he ever was to me.

When I finally found the incredible guy I'm

with now, I was sure it wouldn't last, because he was "too nice to be interesting." Fortunately, I was so exhausted from years of trying to make the wrong guys love me, I relaxed and gave him a chance to show me how remarkably intelligent, likable and lovable he is, how much fun we could have together—and how nice it was to be happy for days, weeks, months on end.

And then the real reason for the "nice guy" problem occurred to me: I actually caught myself thinking, "He's nice to me, but he's nice to everybody! How will I ever know he loves *me*?" Then I realized that young women don't want to be treated like dirt. They want to be treated nicely by guys who aren't nice—guys whose only reason to be nice would be that they were compelled to *change* by their love for that special girl, thus providing her with coveted *proof* of her lovability.

Take a look at nearly every trash novel. The hero is a heartless rake or a villain who only because of his overwhelming love for the heroine *changes* his ways. It's a popular fictional approach to relationships, but it never works in reality, because the guy never *changes*!"

This is the best explanation I've ever come across. It matches my experience. It rings true. Who knows? Who cares? Too nice does not work in the beginning and for an unknown time thereafter.

ONLY COMMODES ACCOMMODATE

Being accommodating is absolutely the kiss of death. You know, adjusting your schedule to hers, agreeing to see the movie she wants after a minor tiff, changing a lunch date because her girl friend is in town.

As stunningly stupid at it sounds, some of them

see you as accommodating if you yield to her desire for Mexican food instead of Chinese!

Commode is spelled like *accommodate.* Use this memory association technique to prevent your affair from ending up in the commode.

Eventually, she may be able to accept your nice treatment of her, phone calls just to talk, flowers, back rubs, presents and so forth. But early on she will simply drop you.

I wish it were not like this, but it is. My helpful hint is simple—Live with it.

Here are some detailed *Helpful Hints* for everyone.

STEELE vs TV SHOWS *Plus! Body Language Video*
Watch me battle Jenny Jones, Jane Whitney, Montel Williams and the ball busters in their audiences. Grace under fire! And a demonstration of how to handle MANIPULATIVE QUESTIONS from women! That's why I teach assertiveness training skills at TRA Workshops. Women are manipulative as a way of life. DEAL WITH IT. After last show, excerpts from TRA workshops and my public lectures show fundamental body language and a few Steel Balls Principles. When I cover how to deal with LET'S JUST BE FRIENDS you will see why it is everyone's favorite bit.

> *Only the amateur*
> *thinks he knows everything.*
> ROBERT LUDLUM
> Response to criticism for using any source in his writing.

Helpful Hints

Keep this knowledge to yourself. Do *not* point out someone's body language and tell them what it means. Why? People will consider you an arrogant showoff. Besides, nobody believes in body language anyway.

SAVE THE SEATS

Women and men, do this on airplanes as you are boarding. Sit on the aisle. Put your property on the window seat to prevent unwanted traveling companions from asking to sit there. When you see someone you want to talk with coming down the aisle, discreetly remove your property, make eye contact and smile.

HOLDING ON

When a couple holds hands, stands arm in arm, or is in constant physical contact with each other at a social gathering, they are saying, neither of us is available. Another interpretation, one of us is afraid the other will go after someone new.

WHERE TO SIT TO MEET SOMEONE

The best way to transmit and receive nonverbal messages is when your eyes can meet and the fronts of your bodies are facing. Choose the seat opposite the person not the one beside him or her. When the group is standing and conversing, put yourself on the opposite side so you are face to face with your potential beloved.

SQUAT DOWN TO BECOME EQUAL

When you meet someone who is sitting, shake hands from the standing position, then squat down to talk. If you continue to stand, the person feels uncomfortable looking up and you are intimidating by being taller. After a few minutes, if the vibes are good, ask "Mind if I sit there and join you?"

SPOTTING GAME-PLAYERS

Women, look for lack of congruence, slickness or over-the-top self-confidence. Men, look for smoothness and lack of fear. Remember, game players often dress the part.

PLAY IS FOREPLAY

Women, when you were young, a boy liked you if he pushed you into the swimming pool or chased you with a bug. Today, when a boy, no matter his age, is interested and he does not know how to tell you, he does something similar.

When an adult male teases or plays with you in a good-hearted manner, consider it foreplay. But, there are some men who tease in a mean, hurtful manner, then try to blame it on you when you take offense. They usually say, "What's the matter with you? I was only joking around." Why? Because they are *bleep*holes.

Men, free-spirited women of all ages also play and tease to initiate courtship. Pay attention.

WIDE WITH DELIGHT

When we see something we like, our pupils dilate to let more of the lovely sight reach our brains. This reaction is involuntary, beyond everyone's control. Several well-known tests have demonstrated how reliable this sign is.

In the most famous test, duplicate photographs of a woman's face were shown to men. The men were asked which shot they preferred. More than 90 percent of the men selected the picture in which the woman's pupils had been air brushed to be slightly larger. When asked why they preferred that picture, not a single man could identify the difference.

During courtship, one of the surest signs of interest is dilated pupils but it's the hardest to become aware of. It's a skill that can be learned if you focus on the other person's eyes. Of course, you can't appear to be staring or gawking.

In another notable experiment, secret, extremely close-up movies were made of men's eyes as they flipped through a stack of photographs. The pictures were placed upside down and included scenic views, children at play, architecture and Playboy centerfolds. Every man's pupils nearly doubled in size when he turned over a photo and confronted a nude beauty.

In poker, if you are dealt a probable winning hand such as a full house, when peeking at the cards, your pupils involuntarily widen to let in that beautiful sight. When expert poker players notice this from across the table they fold their hand to prevent you from winning a bigger pot.

At the World Championship of Poker, shown on ESPN, most professional gamblers wear dark glasses and a hat pulled low over their brow when seated at the table to prevent opponents from seeing their eyes.

FOR WOMEN WHO DON'T SMILE

If it's hard for you to make eye contact and smile, you must learn to do it. As with every other skill you've learned and perfected, it takes practice. Don't begin with men you want attention from. Begin with people who are safe. For example, the service people you meet on a daily basis, at the service station, at the lunch counter, in the grocery store.

Every day, in every possible setting, make eye contact and smile. Walking out of the elevator, depositing your check, while seating yourself in the company cafeteria. Make eye contact and smile. Do it until it's easy and automatic.

DON'T BLIND YOURSELF

As a woman, you must be constantly aware of your intuition, then trust it. Your emotions cannot, and will not, lie to you. But, you can deceive yourself by ignoring your emotions and intuition. That's blinding yourself, then complaining that you could not see he was a dishonest hustler.

SMOKE DETECTOR

Smokers give body language readers an added advantage. The mere act of reaching for a cigarette often indicates reaching for a security blanket or a baby's pacifier. Smoke blown up is confidence. Smoke blown down is lack of confidence, anger or disgust. Tapping a cigarette on the ashtray like a drumstick reveals boredom or mild annoyance. But beating a cigarette on the ashtray angrily is, you guessed it, a sign of anger.

Dragging deeply on a cigarette is often a disguised gasp of astonishment or a method of pausing to gather one's thoughts. At other times it's an attempt to relax by breathing deeply then exhaling deeply.

POSSESSION

Touching means possession and dominance. This is easiest to see in photos of men posing with their new boat, antique car, or even a dead deer.

Putting your feet on your desk, even one foot on the open bottom drawer says, "This is mine."

When someone walks into your office and puts his hands on your property in any manner, he is saying, "I am the real owner of everything in this area, including you!"

Your nonverbal response must be, "Get your damn hands off my stuff!" Reach over, pick up whatever he's fidgeting with. Take possession. Put it where he can't reach it. Don't say anything. Don't explain. You are in charge.

In the library or the cafeteria, putting your purse or briefcase on a table or chair means that piece of furniture and the surrounding area belongs to you.

PHONE-Y-NESS

It's easiest to be lied to on the telephone. All you have to go by are the words, the tone of voice and the pauses. Your eyes get nothing. Beware!

OTHER USES OF BODY LANGUAGE

Encourage your boss to keep talking by *appearing* to listen attentively. Sit up, lean forward, nod, give him a few "uh huh's," raise your eyebrows, tilt your head. Keep your hands off your face and mouth. Don't cross your arms in front of your chest. Don't steeple. Women, don't subconsciously cross and uncross your legs or send any other courtship signals.

Overstaying your welcome in his office makes him see you as dull, inattentive and not getting the work done. When he's done talking, he looks at his watch. If you miss that, he straightens papers, then looks at the papers not at you. If you don't get the hint, he puts his palms on his knees as if he's about to stand. If you're still babbling, he turns his chair and faces the door. If he stands up, you're a dimwit in his eyes.

SEX AND ANTHROPOLOGY

People interested in the biology and evolution of courtship, see *SEX IS NUMBER 4*, in the Appendix. I hope the information there helps each gender understand that the seemingly unnecessary, often hurtful courtship behavior of the opposite sex is frequently beyond the other person's control.

REINFORCED LEARNING

During the coming weeks you are going to become extremely aware of your own body language as well as everyone else's. Great! Why? That information enables you to decide just exactly who's who and what's what.

A couple of days after you finish the main part of this book, read the *Summary* that follows the *Appendix*. Then in a few weeks, read it again. Why? Because as time passes, your subconscious will integrate much of what you will have been observing. Then after you review the fundamentals, you will be able to carry on courtship conversations and you won't have to concentrate so hard on what is being said *without* words. Eventually, you'll be able to relax and let it happen, not make it happen.

Body Language Elaboration covers the details and the finer points you need to discover who she is, then to "tell" her who you are, without words.

This chapter has been added since the first edition was published. The questions and comments are from men who are members of my discussion group on the internet. Women will learn much about men, and themselves, too.

Lengthy excerpts from **OFFICE POLITICS: The Woman's Guide To Beat The System** immediately follow the next chapter.

WARNING! Most women should skip the information after that and proceed directly to the *Appendix* and *Summary*. Why? Because those intervening pages are written by a man for men. It is brutally abrupt and frank. Forewarned is forearmed.

*A woman cannot meet a man, any man,
without thinking, even if it's for half a
second, 'Perhaps this is The man.'*
DORIS LESSING

Body Language Elaboration

This chapter is from my newest book, *Volume II – Advanced Skills, How To Date Young Women For Men Over 35*. It's aimed at guys who have read the first volume. My writing style in those books, and this chapter, is brutally blunt. It may be offensive to some. No offense is intended. It's just how we men talk about women, when you are not around.

Women of all ages can learn a great deal about how we men think, as well as the doubts and struggle we have trying to meet you, then date you.

INTEREST AT A PARTY

Dear Don and Joanna, I especially liked, and learned a lot from the seminar demonstration where she was giving you signals from across the room while conversing in a small group of people. That's exactly the body language Debbie did at the pool where I met her, but she was by herself so I knew what to do!

In that demonstration, you showed us that once mutual signs of interest were exchanged, you signal the desire to talk with her alone by walking toward the group while looking at her and then you veered away and kept walking.

What would be the next thing to do? Would you stop somewhere, examine a painting, and let her make the next move? Guess I've answered my own question.

Steele Sez: You partially answered your own question. Remember, a young woman is strongly concerned about the social danger you pose. That is, she does not want *anyone* in the room to realize that she's considering an older lover. The essence is to communicate with your eyes, as you pass by, that you *are* being discreet and *will be* discreet.

At the party and well afterward, your primary focus is on reassuring her by your casual, not obvious, actions that you will not cause her any social problems.

After passing by, make yourself accessible so that she can approach you when she is able to break out of that group. She may come over and chat, but most likely she will move to a location where she can exchange further non-verbal signals with you in a way that does not attract attention.

From there, follow the step-by-step instructions and strictly adhere to the now famous Ten Commandments of Meeting and Eleven Commandments of Courtship.

SHE'S LOOKING AT MY CROTCH!

This is from a 50 year old who is just getting his find-meet-talk-date-mate legs under him. It's all new, exciting and a bit disorienting because as he told me, "I've been doing everything all wrong for years and years!" Here's what he asked about.

Another good thing your books are doing is increasing my awareness of stuff I never noticed before. I was in the video store last Monday night and for the first time I realized the clerk, a woman of 30, glancing at my crotch. She did it twice quickly. JM, Jersey

Steele Sez: Go back to the store and have something to talk about such as, "Quentin Tarantino, the director of Pulp Fiction, used to work in a place like this. How do you like working here?"

Talk about movies you like. Bid her a fond farewell and as you're parting, say, "See you Thursday." She'll smile and say "Okay," or say, "I don't work Thursday." You say, "So when do you work?" She'll tell you. Nod, smile and leave. Do *not* say that you'll see her on that day. Then, show up on that day and rent a movie.

She'll tell you something about herself if you go first and tell her something about yourself as explained. At the appropriate moment, introduce yourself and shake hands with her.

Don't talk to her for more than a few minutes. You're a busy, important man with places to go and people to see. Compliment her *once* during the conversation about her accessories, jewelry or attire. Pay attention and be aggressive with your eyes to find something you can genuinely say, "That's a very attractive ring! An heirloom?" The compliment must be genuine. If you can't find anything to be genuine about, don't say anything.

Say good bye using her name, "Nice meeting you, Debbie. See ya."

FRENCH SUCCESS STORY

Dear Don, I have been using your techniques very successfully, especially *Body Language Secrets*. I met a 25 year old French girl, Marie. She is beautiful. I ate dinner with her today and really paid attention to her body language.

She sounded happy the whole time, but at times her body language would get very closed. Some of it was when I would talk about subjects that did not interest her. I found that if I also got closed for a while and then opened up, she would too. I believe you talked about this in your book. I was also very laid back and non-aggressive. I was giving off vibrations that I liked her, but I didn't *need* her. I can tell there are good things ahead for me with Marie.

What is your experience with French women? I noticed she is very lively compared to a lot of American girls. I think that French women are more open to go out with older men. Thanks for your help. Steve Dillingham, El Paso

Steele Sez: I have no experience with French females other than when I was in the Army stationed on the French border of Germany. They all stunk, literally! So much for their sophisticated stereotype.

I sincerely believe that women everywhere are the same. However, if she came from France, she has been exposed to *older man-younger woman* possibilities in a positive light, unlike her American "sistahs." So, you will have that going for you. Do not discuss this topic with her until your second anniversary!

Congratulations on maintaining The Right Attitude at dinner. May you continue to maintain it until the end of the fourth month, when you can let it slip a bit, only a bit.

Further congratulations are in order for mastering *Body Language Secrets* and the concept of leading by example and understanding mirroring. I hope readers will have their collective awareness raised by your success in grasping one of the key features of courtship body language. It will also help readers understand the concept of "controlling" the situation by controlling yourself!

GIFTS AND BODY LANGUAGE

Don, There is someone I work with that I am quite fond of. There isn't much office politics involved because it's a part time position.

Whenever we talk, things go great. Unfortunately, there isn't too much opportunity to chat, since it's usually always hectic.

I decided to go out on a limb and buy her a little gift. Nothing big, really, a little chocolate egg with a plastic toy inside.

She really seemed to love it! But I'm wondering if she loved it because someone just gave her a gift, or if it's because the gift was from me. What would be some body language signs I could look out for? No name, please.

Steele Sez: The only way to know if she liked the gift because it was from you is to know if she is interested and attracted to you. The only way to know that, is to interact with her and watch for the signs of interest during conversation.

Study *Body Language Secrets*. Do the homework. Become extremely aware of your own body language. Practice sitting and standing and talking *just as if* you are relaxed, confident, mildly interested and slightly aloof. Pretend you are an actor. Then, practice, practice, practice.

TIP: When you are acutely aware of your own body language, you automatically become acutely aware of everyone else's.

ACCIDENTS DON'T HAPPEN

Don, Help! A woman bumps into me "accidentally" in the bookstore or the grocery store. I know that means she's interested. Tom Paulick, Seattle

Steele Sez: When she indicates interest by touching, wait a moment then smile, nod and say "Finding anything interesting?" Wait. Make certain your body language is open and relaxed. Make certain there are at least four feet between the two of you so that she does not feel threatened.

She will reply to your question with "No!" (fuck off) or "Not yet." (maybe) or she'll say, "Yes," (yes).

From there it is up to you to have something to talk about.

In a bookstore, talk about the books you like that you think women like. For example, body language intrigues most people. Celebrity bios are pretty popular with women.

A good self-revealing statement followed by a question is best. "I came in here to look for a book on John Wayne and I ended up reading this geeky stuff. I'm a programmer, can't help it. What were you looking for?"

As explained in all my books, reveal yourself first, then ask a question. It is important to have some safe, general self-revealing lines and a few general questions for her memorized. That way, the next time one "accidentally" bumps you, you're ready. Vince Lombardi and I do not believe in luck.

I can guarantee you that unless you're as suave as Cary Grant, as handsome as Tom Selleck, or as manly as Paul Newman, don't attempt humor or a flirty remark. Start out easy, you can always come on hard.

EYE CONTACT BASICS

Dennis asked how young women show their interest from across the room.

Steele Sez: Longer than socially appropriate eye contact indicates interest. Smiles signal, "Come over here and talk with me. I don't bite."

Your response to her long look is to smile and nod to acknowledge her existence. That also lets her know that you are interested. When she smiles back, go over and talk with her. Use the direct approach when you get there, "Hi. I'm Dennis. What's your name?" as you extend your hand to shake with her. There are about 40 other ways to tell when she's interested.

NECK TOUCHING LANGUAGE

This is from a recently divorced guy of 38 who is starting to "hear" what women say without words.

After reading your super *Body Language Secrets,* I have become extremely aware of women's signals. The woman I was talking with was touching and fingering the top buttons on her blouse, up by the neck. Is this the same as touching the necklace, or is it symbolic undressing?

Steele Sez: Necklace touching most likely. It always depends on the cluster of gestures surrounding the signal. I'm glad to hear you are becoming aware of what women are "saying" without words, but you are making the mistake everyone does when first mastering this information. I made it when I began. The mistake is that you zero in on one signal or gesture and focus on it.

Remember, one signal means nothing. Even two signals cannot be relied on. You must look for clusters of three or more signals. When she sends you three signals of interest in a row, that means she's interested.

Back to a woman fiddling with the top buttons on her blouse. That usually is a sign that you are coming on too strong or you may be too close physically. When you notice any sort of neck touching, immediately but diplomatically change the subject of conversation and move slightly back. She was signaling that she needs reassurance of your motives and sincere interest.

Master the concept of looking for clusters. Learn to notice one signal, then search for similar signals that follow the one you noticed.

Fine Point: When she's undecided, she sends mixed nonverbal signals even though she's smiling. This means you are doing okay. Keep it lightweight and superficial while sending nonverbal, positive signals of interest to her. Then, as I preach, *let* it happen.

SPREADS HER LEGS

This is from 40 year old Matt. He just finished reading *Body Language Secrets*.

My question is whether her posture and body language said something that should have triggered me to do something, like go over and talk with her.

As I walked back into the coffee section of the bookstore, I noticed the sexually enticing posture of a young wire-rimmed-glasses-wearing cutie. She was absorbed in her reading as I came within eye-shot. She was relaxed and reclined in her chair, about to slide off. Her legs spread 45 degrees, her tight jeans hugging her crotch with real evidence of labial contours in the denim. Yummy!

Is this the same as explained in *Body Language Secrets* when a woman faces you with the front of her body. You said this is evolution in action offering a sexual display of breast and crotch. If not, could she be nothing more than a tease? If not, does this unladylike posture indicate sexual arousal?

Answer 1: No, spreading her legs is not even remotely similar to facing you with the front of her body when she's sitting or standing. Spreading her legs and slouching in the chair indicates nothing more than being relaxed, comfortable, and confident and thus, unaware of her unladylike posture.

Comment 1: Any female who wears her jeans so tight that you can count her pubic hairs wants you to look at her pubic hairs.

Answer 2: She could be nothing more than a tease or she could be trolling for men by advertising her figure. In my lifetime, 90 percent of women who dress in sweaters, jeans or whatever that are tight-enough-to-draw-a-second look, are teases, thus they are of no interest to me. Or, they are so immature they don't realize how ridiculous they look, thus, they are of no interest to me.

Answer 3: That posture does not indicate sexual arousal. Being turned on is indicated by "high courtship readiness" postures and gestures as explained and shown in the photos, of *Body Language Secrets.*

SHE'S MAKING EYES AT ME!

That's an old saying but I don't know what it means. I've heard it described as a repeated, rapid dilation of the eyes. Bill Taylor, Orange CA

Steele Sez: Dilation is a strong sign of attraction! However, it is difficult for men to consciously notice, except for expert poker players.

I remember the expression meaning, "He's flirting with his eyes." That is, giving strong, direct but friendly eye contact. His pupils may be dilated, but that's not the power. It is epitomized by Clark Gable as Captain Rhett Butler. With his head slightly tilted, he gave a manly glance with a pleased look on his face plus slightly raising his eyebrows in acknowledgment of the woman's beauty and presence.

Bill Sez: It also seems to be a learned and controlled function.

Steele Sez: Dilation is involuntary, impossible to control.

Bill Sez: I simply remember it as the warm and tingly feeling I used to get when looking deeply into a woman's eyes.

Steele Sez: That reaction is from becoming vulnerable to her vulnerability. Wonderful, but nothing to do with dilation. Being seen and seeing is what romantic mental health is all about. Knowing what you know and seeing what you see is what self-confidence is all about. Self-confidence, genuine self-confidence is what makes you attractive, sensual and sexual to women of all ages.

That's genuine self-confidence not the put on kind, not an act, not phony. The real thing. You get it from being successful and relaxed. Women spot it at 100 yards, just by the way you walk and carry yourself.

Bill Sez: I only notice it today in sincere lovers, but that can be really brief.

Steele Sez: Brief because it is so intense and most of us cannot stand too much intensity. I, myself, prefer intensity! It makes living in the *now* much easier as well as making each day memorable, as opposed to the way the days were all alike before I got divorced! To enjoy intensity, one must experience it over and over. Slowly, one realizes that intense pain *and* intense joy are what makes life worth living! By the way, you can't have one without the other! It's all or nothing.

Bill Sez: I confess to using it to try to warm up some interesting women.

Steele Sez: Not a good idea! Trying to see into her soul is an invasion and she'll react to it like that. When you relax and let down your walls, most women react positively and reciprocate almost immediately.

In other words, you have to go first and make yourself open and vulnerable. First with your body language, second with your tone of voice, third by your attitude of being relaxed *and* confident. It takes courage and practice to become vulnerable, but that's where it's at, my friend.

Women! Get *OFFICE POLITICS: The Woman's Guide To Beat The System.* In the next chapter, I describe it. *OP* is also extremely useful for men under 40 because 90 percent of it applies to guys.

APPENDIX

NOTE 1 BRAIN WIRING

Women's renowned intuition arises from the way biology and evolution "wired" female brains. The connection between the left half and the right half of the female brain is much larger in women than it is in men.

Much to the displeasure of radical feminists, physical differences between male and female brains, as well as bodies, explain most, if not all, gender-specific talents and capabilities.

Evolution wired female brains differently. That causes them to have a different world-view as well as different perceptions of everyday reality, courtship and romantic relationships.

Women's ability to notice extremely small changes makes them far more (40%) proficient at caring for infants as well as gathering food and supplies for the clan.

Even an inexperienced woman can notice extremely minute changes in a newborn's facial expression and color as well as minuscule changes in breathing rate and body temperature. This enables a mother to recognize what the baby needs without the child being able to speak. Obviously, this ability was, is, *and always will be,* necessary for survival of homo sapiens.

But, women don't efficiently process strictly rational, spatial information that arises in the left brain because the larger connection allows interference from the right brain. This causes a lesser ability to find their way in the wild, or in today's world, to understand maps and blueprints.

The smaller connection in men makes them far more proficient (40%) at hitting a target with a thrown object, such as a spear. This clearly makes men far better hunters and warriors. It also accounts for men's vastly superior ability in spatial relations, a mandatory prerequisite to becoming a draftsman, engineer or wilderness guide.

Differences in ability are scientifically demonstrable from the age of two!

TIME, 1-20-92, *Sizing Up the Sexes,* Christine Gorman. SCIENTIFIC AMERICAN, 9-92, *Sex Differences in the Brain,* Doreen Kimura.

NOTE 2 ABNORMAL HAPPENS

Females of every single species of mammal except one refuse to mate with non-aggressive males. That species is our own, homo sapiens.

Passive males, and the women who seek them, are products of a non-natural world, our world, the civilized, industrialized, capitalistic Western World.

In the natural world of hunter-gather bands, a non-aggressive male usually starves to death. Even if he doesn't, no female will mate with him. Thus his passive characteristics are never passed on.

In our world, parents do not *need* children to help with hunting and gathering as our distant ancestors did. In our world, parents do not *need* children to help with the endless physical labor needed to survive on a single-family farm as our great-great grandparents did.

This means that some parents can, and do, behave toward their children in ways that are heartless, erratic, stressful, abusive. In simple terms, crazy as well as unnatural.

These children develop survival tactics as they

attempt to meet their normal, natural needs for touching, loving and self esteem in their insane universe.

When they become adults, as compared with most people, they have a different world-view, have different ways of relating to the opposite sex and have different expectations of the opposite sex. At the same time, these people are trying to meet the unmet needs of childhood.

Men who became passive to survive, often choose a strong, controlling woman who resembles their deranged mother. It is a futile attempt to get from a wife what his mother did not give him. And, women who survived often seek a man who resembles their unsound father in an attempt to get what they did not get as a child.

Other women who survived seek a passive man they can control and manipulate so they are never, ever abused and hurt again.

In our world, an unnatural world, a passive male does not starve to death and neither does the type of female who seeks him out. These aberrant couples sometimes produce a child. To understate it, their child's long-range genetic future is not bright.

NOTE 3 SEX IS NUMBER FOUR

I hope this section helps each gender understand that the seemingly unnecessary, often hurtful courtship behavior of the opposite sex is frequently beyond the other person's control.

Remember Maslow's hierarchy of needs from Psychology 101? Air is the most important. Water is second. Food is third. Fourth, comes sex, even before security, which is fifth. Love is sixth. Self actualization last.

Once the need for air is satisfied, one seeks water until that need is satisfied. Food then becomes the dominate need. If one has enough to eat, sex is the driving force, even at the office, even at the beach, even when socializing (courting) after church.

ANTHROPOLOGIST'S VIEW

In an interview with Playboy, anthropologist Helen Fisher, PhD, author of *The Natural History of Monogamy, Adultery and Divorce* answered this question. I was delighted she said what I had written.

What do you think about this constant harangue over the issue of patriarchy?

Naomi Wolf came out with that ridiculous book, *The Beauty Myth*, in which she blames men and the entire advertising industry for the fact that women want to remain beautiful and thin all their lives.

But for millions of years, men have been attracted to women who look youthful. That was an evolutionary adaptive response because clear eyes, white teeth, smooth skin and a youthful appearance indicated that the woman was more likely to have fresher eggs and more likely to bear viable young. As a result, men have always been attracted to women who look healthy and young.

If the New York advertising, cosmetic and clothing industries fell into the Hudson River, women would re-create them, because the human female instinctively seeks to look youthful, healthy and attractive. That has nothing to do with patriarchy.

MEN HAVE ALWAYS BEEN DIFFERENT

After three decades of feminist propaganda a few men and many women believe that males and females are the same. They choose to ignore that during the rise of mammals over the past 60 million years, evolution perfected the male homo sapiens and perfected the female homo sapiens. Survival dictated the essential characteristics of each gender.

Males developed characteristics that are best for the survival of everyone in a hunter-gatherer band of about 25 humans. Females developed characteristics that are best for the survival of everyone in a hunter-gatherer band of 25 humans.

Survival determined that males must be aggressive and competitive. Survival determined that females must be nurturing and submissive, unless defending their young. Every human male and every human female has these fundamental gender characteristics.

Characteristics developed over millions of years do not disappear when civilization arises. And, these gender differences do not disappear just because the corporation or the singles' bar or the condo owner's committee is not a hunter-gatherer band.

BLINK OF A GEOLOGIC EYE

We homo sapiens created today's civilization in only 10,000 years. But we took 60 million years to become homo sapiens. Just under our thin skin of Western culture, we are the same as we have been for millions upon millions of years.

To understand the *natural* principles of courtship, the principles that really control us, it is necessary to understand evolutionary, biological human nature—not the human nature professed by parents, priests and politicians.

BARBARIANS IN WAITING

Here in the United States, the most advanced country in the world, civilized behavior hangs by a thread. Doubt that?

Admit that everyday people rob the dead at an airliner crash. Think back on the Rodney King riots. Recall that many of the looters were average citizens. And, if still in doubt, go for a walk by yourself, unarmed, on the *wrong side of town* in any major city after midnight.

When there is no fear of retribution, many people become instant barbarians. If lawlessness persists, all of us must defend ourselves with force or be devoured, just as it was before civilization. Why? We are the same as we have always been.

So what? You ask. Well, if you realize that we are the same creatures we have always been, you can see that courtship is not exactly what we have been led to believe by our society and its institutions.

GENUINE, FUNDAMENTAL COURTSHIP

The principle goal evolution built into each of us is the same—*get your DNA into the future.* Each of us wants to, in a sense, live forever. That's exactly what we do when we send our DNA, in the form of a replica of ourselves, into the future.

The woman offers the man the ability to send a replica of himself into the future. The man offers the woman the ability to send a replica of herself into the future. At this point, men always ask, *so, if that's the case, can't we just skip all these courtship games?* Let's look at our ancestors to understand.

ANSWERS FROM ANCIENT ANCESTORS

We are all descendants of people who lived brutish, nasty, bloody, short lives, less than 25 years. Infants had to be suckled at the mother's breast for nearly four years.

FEMALE STRATEGY

Then, as now, a woman's goal is different for physical and biological reasons. She doesn't just want to get her DNA into the future, but to get it there with the best chance for survival. The key phrase is "best chance for survival."

Men, look at our hunter-gather ancestors and realize that it's in a woman's best interest (in the evolutionary sense) to be persuaded only by strong, healthy, high-status males. Why? Her evolutionary programming tells her she must devote four years to nursing each child she produces before she can become pregnant again. (Suckling causes women to produce a hormone that prevents pregnancy.)

In short, on a fundamental, evolutionary level she knows she has only a *few chances* to get a replica of herself into the future. Thus, it is crucial that her replica have the best possible chance for survival. That's why she is particular. That's why you must persuade her.

In everyday terms, evolution wants a woman to be picky. Evolution wants her to select a strong, healthy male who is capable of providing food and protection for her and the child. When our grandparents described that male, they referred to him as "a good father and provider." At the dawn of the 21st century he's called a "great catch."

MALE STRATEGY

Women, let's look at our hunter-gatherer ancestors to understand men. In the evolutionary sense, it is in a man's best interest to persuade as many women as possible. Why? After adolescence, he produces millions of sperms every day until he dies, and any single one can send his replica into the future. The more women he persuades, the more replicas he sends. The more replicas of him there are, the better the chances that at least one will survive.

HERE WE ARE, AS WE WERE

Today, we are fundamentally the same mammals who scavenged for carcasses of animals killed by carnivores 250,000 years ago. Yet here we are, a quarter of a million years later eyeing each other across the dance floor at a wedding reception.

High status males at the reception have a far wider selection of females to choose from than males of low status.

TODAY'S HIGH STATUS MALES

The high status males of our hunter-gatherer ancestors were men who could provide the things necessary for survival in that culture—food and safety. Thus, the best hunter-warriors had first choice of the females.

They selected females, replicated themselves and moved into the future. We are the result of those high status males and the desirable females they chose. Their DNA is the foundation of our DNA. They indelibly stamped their characteristics into our being. Their blood runs within us, literally. We are them. They are us.

Today, high status males are men who can provide the things necessary for survival in this culture—food and safety, just as with hunter-gatherers.

We don't live in small bands where everyone knows who the high-status males are, but that's not a problem for our society's males of the highest possible status: movie stars, rock stars, athletic stars, political stars and stars of finance and industry.

> *I tried to accommodate*
> *as many young ladies as possible.*
> MAGIC JOHNSON

All across the country everyone knows who they are because of mass communication. Thus, our highest status males can pick and choose which females they mate with no matter where they are.

That's until they want to mate with our society's most desirable females. Then, they too, must woo those females. Why? Because other high status males want those women too. Universal, fundamental fact—males compete, the victors get to choose.

Our society's other very high status males let females know who they are by displaying:

Expensive, exotic automobiles, yachts, aircraft
Expensive, fashionable attire and accessories
Expensive homes in prestigious neighborhoods
Expensive gifts to highly desirable women.

The operative word is *expensive.* Money buys food, shelter, safety and long term security for the female and the children. Among this group of males, there is competition for the most desirable females. As always, the winners get to choose.

And so it goes, on down the socio-economic ladder. Within each income group, males compete for the most desirable females in their group. It is no different from our hunter-gatherer ancestors. The best hunter-warrior got first choice. The second best got second choice and so on. Survival of the fittest.

The most desirable females selected by victorious males in every culture have always had the same two outstanding attributes. Hugh Hefner capitalized on that fact, sold it to males of all ages, and became a billionaire.

THE MOST DESIRABLE FEMALES

Females selected by high status males in all cultures since the beginning of homo sapiens invariably have the same two attributes:

(1) FERTILITY
(2) PROLIFIC REPRODUCTIVE CAPABILITY

In today's culture, just as in the culture of our hunter-gatherer ancestors, age and physical condition identifies the most desirable females. They all have these attributes:

Trim, strong bodies
White, sound teeth
Hands with tight skin
Upright, firm breasts

Lustrous, clear finger nails
Faces with smooth, clear skin
Solid buttocks and flat stomachs
Bright eyes with extremely clear whites.

ADVERTISING HER INTEREST

We humans cherish the belief that we are different from animals. This commonly held view says that we have free will and thus are in control of our destiny and our behavior.

Yet each month, the human female's brain chemistry and body chemistry change for a few days. She thinks differently. She acts differently. She even dresses differently.

The shift occurs as her egg breaks away from the ovary and begins its descent down the fallopian tube. It's ovulation—the homo sapiens variation of mammalian estrus—coming into heat. Only during this brief time during the month, can she send her DNA into the future.

Robert Wright, in *The Moral Animal*, investigates free will versus evolutionary determinism. Wright presents convincing evidence that evolution controls far more of our individual lives than we care to admit or even examine.

A scientific study, cited by Wright, documented that ovulating young women subconsciously dress to expose far more skin at events with courtship possibilities than non-ovulating young women. Ovulating females wear deeper necklines, higher hemlines, shorter sleeves as well as bare midriffs and backs.

One last time, y*ou cannot not communicate.*

Simplify, simplify

HENRY DAVID THOREAU

Summary

People form 90 percent of their opinion about you in the first 90 seconds. Nonverbal signals have five times more impact than verbal signals. In particular, your appearance communicates. The way you are dressed dictates how others respond to you.

You cannot not communicate. No matter what you do, or don't do, you broadcast your emotional state. Everything is body language—tone of voice, clearing our throats, rubbing our eyes, crossing our arms, tapping our toes, touching our nose—everything except the words we say.

Only clusters of gestures are reliable. Single, individual gestures are not.

WHO'S WHO

A genuine person is nervous and excited when meeting you. Genuine people are somewhat awkward and childish no matter how hard they try to be cool and relaxed.

Rapo and *Cavalier* players want sexual gratification without emotional involvement. Their trademark—poised and relaxed instead of excited and nervous. Sharply dressed, attractive, smooth talkers are practiced experts.

Openness is sincerity because the speaker, or listener, has nothing to hide. Doubt the words of anyone whose feet are not flat on the floor and steady. The liar often moves his hands toward his mouth or eyes during or immediately after the lie. Talking from behind a wall of hands indicates lying or being extremely cau- tious with his choice of words.

Actions speak louder than words.

Believe what people do, **not** what they say.

SIGNS OF INTEREST

Joanna was lovingly stroking the long stem up and down, up and down. Women, don't hesitate to use this powerful signal to tell the man he's doing just fine. Men, the equivalent is to run your finger slowly around the rim of your glass.

Women, if you are interested, break off sustained eye contact by looking down before looking away. This your first act of submission and the first sign of reassurance that he will not be hurt if he comes over and talks with you.

Frequency of eye contact, the more the better. Amount of time she, or he, holds your gaze, the longer the better. How *she* breaks off eye contact, down before away is great! Shine of the eyes, the brighter the better. Direction of body, toward you, good, away, bad. Overall posture, erect and alert are good. Tilt of head, vertical is bad, increased tilt is great. Where the drink is held, high in front as a barrier, that's bad. Hand activity, clenched, squeezing or pinching is bad, open, caressing or stroking is great.

FINDING

Do *not* try to find him, or her, any place where peo- ple try to meet: bars, clubs, spas.

During courtship, *subconsciously*, all of us tend to adopt the same posture as the person we are inter- ested in. When man teases or plays, consider it fore- play. Free-spirited women of all ages also play to initi- ate courtship.

Acknowledge her, or him, every time you have the chance. Say "Hi," nod and smile on your way to, or from. the rest room, bar, kitchen or pool. You're just being friendly. These "Hi's" are first conversations. You won't be a stranger when you start the second conversation.

Helpful Hint. At all gatherings, never park yourself for long any place. Circulate. If you must stop for awhile, sooner or later, everyone passes through the kitchen. It's a great place to watch the body language as you watch the traffic.

The woman who brazenly exhibits her physical as-sets will get the attention of every man in the room, initially. After a short time, most men lose interest. To strongly attract, and then hold a man's attention and interest, you must have a secret.

Anticipation is arousing. Be secretive. Be sugges-tive. Be almost-but-not-quite. Lure us with the un-known. Imply there's much more than meets our eye.

You have the power to attract him and at the same time to reassure him. Eye contact followed by a smile is the most effective attention getter any woman has. When you look at a man and smile, you nonverbally say, *"Hi! How ya doin'. I'm friendly. I don't bite."*

MEETING

The touching that takes place when shaking hands enables your emotions and subconscious to make lightning like value judgments. Massive amounts of genuine data are exchanged as the two of you touch. What you both learn is gut knowledge—who the other person *really* is.

As a woman you have the power to send discreet and distinct, yet potent, signals without words. The most powerful thing you can do is touch him. It makes no difference when, how, where or why. Communicate your motives, your wants, your needs, your dislikes as well as your limits, simply by the way you touch a man. Use what you have.

Do NOT go over and talk to the first or even the second one who smiles at you. Smile back. Circulate. Send out signals. Notice the signals women are send-ing you. Take your time.

Nowadays women do not trust any man. It is nor-mal for a woman to test you.

TALKING

Courtship is attraction, supplication, stimulation, fascination, exhilaration, inspiration, titillation, but most of all it is—PERSUASION.

We humans conduct courtship by talking, but most communicating is done with facial expression, tone of voice, posture and the manner of touching.

The essence of courtship conversations is to communicate, with and without words. *This is who I am. I like myself. I hope you do too. Tell me about yourself so I can discover if I like you.*

When you do and say the right things during the critical first moments, the moments turn into minutes. Only after she has discovered (1) you are safe and (2) interesting, can she find you attractive

To persuade her, you must reveal yourself so she can decide. Talk about what you like and dislike as you give her plenty of openings to do the same thing. The key is giving her information about you, so she'll give you information about herself, then you'll have something to talk about.

When you're *not* trying, you have The Right Attitude.

DATING

What is a date? The next to last step of courtship. It's any activity undertaken in the pretext of having fun that gives the female time to decide, consciously or subconsciously, if she has been persuaded.

A successful date (persuasion is happening) has a rhythm to it. Anticipation, excitement and arousal come and go. They intermingle with pleasant relaxation and enjoyable conversation, which, in turn, are replaced by anticipation and arousal.

Avoid controversial subjects. Reveal your likes and dislikes in movies, sports, food, travel, drinks, games, and such. Arranging a second date is much easier after finding out where you two fit together. Mention things you like to do and places you like to go.

Men, not being too nice is a mandatory, all inclusive

mandate you must follow to have The Right Attitude. Who knows? Who cares? Too nice does not work in the beginning and for an unknown time thereafter.

Commode is spelled like *accommodate*. Use this memory association technique to prevent your affair from ending up in the commode.

As a woman, you must be constantly aware of your intuition, and then trust it. Your emotions cannot, and will not, lie to you. But, you can deceive yourself by ignoring your emotions and intuition. That's blinding yourself, and then complaining that you could not see he was a dishonest hustler.

As a man, you are being evaluated by a woman who has an infallible truth detecting device, her intuition. Don't lie. As a woman, don't deny yourself the greatest means you have of knowing if he's telling the truth. Use your intuition and trust it.

THE LISTS

Here's a summary of the gestures liars use:

SPEAK NO EVIL	TOUCHES MOUTH
SEE NO EVIL	TOUCHES EYE
HEAR NO EVIL	TOUCHES EAR
FEEL NO EVIL	UNGROUNDED FEET

From across the room, these are the Signs Of Interest in the approximate courtship sequence.

I'M INTERESTED	DON'T BOTHER ME
Sidelong glance(s)	Never sneaks a peek
Looks at you a few times	Fleeting eye contact
Holds your gaze briefly	Looks away quickly
Downcast eyes, then away	Looks away, eyes level
Posture changes to alert	Posture unchanged
Preens, adjusts hair, attire	Does no preening
Turns body toward you	Turns body away
Tilts head	Head remains vertical
Narrows eyes slightly	Eyes remain normal
Twists, tugs at ring	Shows ring-back of hand
Smiles	Neutral, polite face
Matches your posture	Posture unchanged

Eyes sparkle	Normal or dull eyes
Licks her lips	Keeps mouth closed
Moves hand to her hip	Posture unchanged
Thrusts breasts	Sags to de-emphasize breasts

SEVEN THINGS WOMEN WANT

(1) Don't be pushy. I'm not good at telling people to buzz off.

(2) Don't be obvious, although I may be interested, I don't want everyone in the room to know.

(3) Even if this is fun and exciting, I may be a bit nervous.

(4) Don't show you're nervous, it makes me nervous. Be casual, friendly and relaxed. It'll help me stay that way.

(5) Keep the conversation superficial, further into it, leave a few openings for me to tactfully indicate how we're doing and if I want to continue or not.

(6) Later on, when I'm more sure of myself, don't ask for too much. Give me room to maneuver to save face, mine and yours.

(7) If I turn you down, don't act like a jerk because you started this.

First conversation—these are the signals that tell you what to do. Women only indicated by italics:

KEEP TALKING	MOVE ON
Alert, energetic	Tense, restless
Pupils dilated	Normal or small pupils
Gradually opens posture	Posture remains closed
Lowers drink	Keeps drink chest high
Touches self gently	Grips or pinches self
Caresses objects	Squeezes, taps objects
Crosses and uncrosses legs	*Legs remain crossed*
Flashes of palm	*Back of hand gestures*
Crossed legs steady	Swings crossed legs
Dangles shoe on toe	*Keeps shoe on*
Hands never touch face	Touches face
Touches you any reason	*Never touches you*
Feet firmly on floor	Feet on edges or toes
Loosens anything	Tightens anything

| Leans forward | Leans away |
| Steady hands, feet | Tapping, drumming |

During subsequent conversations, these are the signals that tell you what to do:

YOU'RE DOING GREAT!	ONLY BEING POLITE
Keeps eyes on you	Looks around room
Head tilts farther	Head only slightly tilted
Smiles broadly and often	Smiles slightly
Hands open, relaxed	Hands closed
Puts anything in mouth	Nothing goes in mouth
Posture changes to yours	Maintains posture
Turns body toward you	Keeps body facing away
Sucks straw, looks at you	*Looks away and drinks*
Removes eyeglasses	Puts on eyeglasses

YOU'RE COMING ON TOO STRONG

Averts her eyes	Looks around room
Nervous smile	Touches her face or head
Leans or backs away	Turns front of body away
Touches throat, necklace	Picks at hand or finger
Moves head to vertical	Hands begin to clench, grip
Begins to fidget	Raises drink in front of her

THAT'S ENOUGH, GO AWAY!

Looks away often	Shifts posture, turns away
Becomes tense	Stops smiling, starts frowning
Brushes imaginary lint	Sits up straight
Crosses arms, legs	Picks up drink
Locks ankles under chair	Hands close, clench

Drums fingers, swings leg, taps foot.

Here's how you communicate The Right Attitude without words.

SLIGHTLY ALOOF	HIGHLY INTERESTED
Sometimes open posture	All openness
Usually body angled away	Body facing her
Rarely lean toward her	Always lean toward her
Neutral or pleasant face	Moderately serious
Preen now and again	Preen often
Relaxed posture	Erect, ready posture

Rarely touch her	Touch as often as possible
Polite smiles	Broad smiles
Occasional, intense eye contact	Look her in the eyes
Caress yourself once	Caress yourself regularly
Hold your glass steady	Finger glass sensually

SIGNS OF BOREDOM

Looking at wristwatch	Doodling
Asking what time it is	Drumming fingertips
Tapping foot	Swinging leg
Blank stare	Head in hand
Drooped eyelids	Hand on side of face or head

SIGNS OF SUPERIORITY AND ARROGANCE

Steepling	Looking down one's nose
Nose in the air	Peering over one's glasses
Hands behind back	Feet on desk or coffee table
Hands on back of head	Examines one's cuticles
Arms crossed on chest	Patronizing compliments
Fatherly pats	Snorting through nose

Videos, Books MP3s, Audio CDs

INTERACT DIRECTLY WITH DON VIA EMAIL Since 1997 Don's on-line Steel Balls Discussion Group had delivered INSTANT SOLUTIONS to your problems. A few of the 100+ members were right where you are only a short time ago. They share how they got on down the Road to Success in Dating. Click DISCUSSION at *www.rdonsteele.com*

3 DISK SET Body Language And Success With Women
At a special workshop Don and Joanna worked with 24 guys from age 20 to 65! Don shows and explains the whats and whys of Body Language. Joanna tells you something only a young woman knows as she demonstrates key signs of interest and disinterest from across the room and when engaged in verbal intercourse. See it. Understand it. Master this new "lingo." On the third disk it is all Joanna. She is spectacular! Frank! Funny! Bold! Honest! She presents her views on no no's, hair, teeth and any subject the guys wanted to hear about. She ranged from a sex with young women through toupees, SUVs, pickup trucks, t-shirts, jeans, sideburns, music, hair dyes, long hair, sports cars, earrings, Dockers, penny loafers, and on and on.

2-DISK SET The Right Attitude Workshop
Never before seen. Inside Steele's The Right Attitude workshop. It's all there for you! 24 hours of video distilled to the essence of The Right Attitude:

LOOK LIKE A MAN Power Suit Fundamentals
WALK LIKE A MAN T Babes and RDS show you how
TALK LIKE A MAN Coached by Joanna, Savann and Roxie 'nuff said!

Brutal honesty about sex, seduction, pick up no no's, even your pets! Directly from the Titanium Babes during the most popular event of the workshop *Open Forum* aka ask us anything, ANY-DAMN-THING!. Extensive explanation, demonstation and role playing of Steele's realistic techniques to: Find, Meet, Talk, Date, Relate. Move from the couch to the bedroom is the climax of Disk 2.

2-DISK SET Body Language and Steel Balls Principles
When learning body language a single picture is worth 1000 words. To really *understand* body language a moving picture is worth 10,000

words. These vcds make it possible for you to become an expert in noticing HER body language as well as mastering fundamental Steel Balls Principles. There is a machine gun summary. Compressed, thus AMPLIFIED. Extremely informative as well as funny and entertaining!

STEELE ON THE RADIO! 30-hour MP3 CDs
That's right 30 hours long! Entertaining, funny as well as powerfully informative! From Steele's call-in talk radio show. Solve common problems, master the finer points of dating and find out what Don learned the hard way. First volume has 4 videos and plays only on a computer. Volumes 2 and 3 play on newer mp3 players.

STEELE ON NATIONAL TELEVISION 2 disk Video
Jenny Jones, Jane Whitney, Montel Williams and the ball busters in their audiences do their best to make Don look bad. To Tell The Truth shows you how I use what Don knows to . . . you'll see! Dick Clark's The Other Half. More attempts to make Older Men Younger Women look bad. See how Don handled them!

ARTS & ENTERTAINMENT, *Seminar, Interviews* 2 disk Video
A&E crew taped us for a national hour-long show on Older-Younger. The best part is a mini seminar Joanna and I conducted. We prepared three guys to attend a reception at a local art gallery, young women, provided by A&E. During rehearsal and the real, on-camera seminar, Joanna covered shoes, slacks, shirts, sideburns, hair cuts/styles, unbuttoning shirts and shirt sleeves, teeth, sunglasses, shorts, tank tops, colors for shirts and on and on. I covered What Do You Have That She Wants, body language basics.

HOW TO DATE YOUNG WOMEN
Brutal honesty that works no matter how old your are or how young or old she is from a man who has dated young women for the past thirty years. Steele tells you bluntly who she is, where she is, then how to meet, talk with and date her. He tells you bluntly who she is, where she is, then how to meet, talk with and date her. Years of success-failure stories and a provocative, yet sensitive style make this book an enjoyable read.

HOW TO DATE–*Volume II Advanced Skills*
Steele forcefully expands his kickass, no-nonsense approach. He has included a lengthy chapter, *For Married Men Over 35!* 352 pages. *Volume II* is strictly for buyers of *How To Date Young Women.*

SEXPECTATIONS: *Women Talk Frankly About Sex And Dating*
It got a kickass review by *Playboy.* Strong reinforcement of the knowledge and understanding developed from Volume 1 and 2. You will grasp firmly what she thinks and believes about sex and sexuality. Some very ROUGH stuff from older women into weird sex. Guys have complained to me! Don't read those parts if you are offended. The

main benefit is getting reinforcement and verification right from the females we are interested in: girl-next-door types and the intelligent young women that I discuss and prefer.

A MAN'S GUIDE TO WOMEN
I love this book no matter how geeky. It's full of useful data at only 80 pages long! A powerful package of fundamental data. It's *mandatory* for guys who are inexperienced or recently divorced.

THREESOME: *How To Fulfill Your Favorite Fantasy*
70% more women buy this than men! 232 pages of reality: how, who, when, where, what to do to arrange a ménage a trois. Actual, practical, realistic and based on experience. She reveals all the methods and techniques she has used for the past 15 years. Stop dreaming. MAKE it happen.

DATING 101 - The instant Cure for Romance Blues.
This book was written by two women who have a proven track record. Zella Case, a professional matchmaker since 1968 has 500 marriages to her credit! Melissa Darnay worked as a professional match maker and singles consultant and lectures at seminars & workshops to help people find love & happiness. Discover the secrets of how to find, attract and date your soul mate.

ONE-HOUR ORGASM – Learn the Butterfly Technique
One of only five books by others that I will sell. Why? Because the book was written by two famous sex therapists who KNOW what they are talking about. For men and women. It works! This book will change your love life forever.

PLAYGIRL INTERVIEW audio CD 74 minutes
Don talks with the Managing Editor of Playgirl, Cheri, Hawk and Live Young Girls. BONUS! One hour of Steele's outrageous, informative, take-no-prisoners advice on find, meet, talk, date, mate.

BBC INTERVIEWS STEELE 90 minute audio tape
Bravo's Louis Theroux's Weird Weekend's producer talked with me for two hours. This guy is the best interviewer on the planet! He had me explain everything I do, how I do it, why I do it, covered my years with Nathaniel Branden. Everything you wanted to know about me!

REINFORCE AUDIO CD SET
Steele reinforces your knowledge as he entertains you! Don edited the best of 200 radio interviews into an exciting, easy way to master this skill. Fundamentals are amplified. Humor is rampant.. When you listen Steel Balls Principles are r-e-i-n-f-o-r-c-e-d First you read then see the videos now as you hear it, everything gets reinforced as the radio show hosts ask Don the right questions to help you focus on the key points. Find, meet, talk, skills re-emphasized. Clothes, haircut,

cologne, cars, jewelry. Identify gold diggers, cockteasers, RAPO players. Meeting and Courtship commandments. Bars, nightclubs, on and on! Two Audio CDs 74 minutes each.

THE RIGHT ATTITUDE WORKSHOP

R. Don Steele and several young women run a workshop where you learn in a controlled, safe atmosphere, where nobody is embarrassed or ridiculed. You learn by doing, then getting feedback, the fastest way to develop these crucial skills.

Body Language at Distance	*Move To The Bedroom*
Complimenting Her	*Phone Calls Check list*
Conversation- Body Language	*Rapo Players*
Ending The First Date	*Returning Phone Calls*
First Date Conversation	*Reveal Yourself*
Her Complaints	*Set Up A First Get Together*
Inevitable Questions	*She Doesn't Call*
Leaving Messages	*Using Her Self Revelations*
Let's Just Be Friends	*When To Kiss Her*
LUST In Your Eyes	*When To Move On*

Detailed information on TRA Workshop at www.rdonsteele.com

HIGH LEVEL WORKSHOPS

Many graduates of The Right Attitude workshop attend our other workshops. As the grads know, your clothes must be sensual and sexy so that the woman wants to rip them off!

Dress for Successful Dating. 3-days only eight guys get detailed info on how to select and wear attire for: Coffee Date, Lunch or Pizza and Beer Date, Sports Date and a Romantic Date. On Friday morning our expert take you to an upscale salon where she and the owner develop a new hairstyle for you that's makes you as manly as possible. That's followed by a day long shopping expedition under her direction. Saturday and Sunday are spent on learning how to coordinate and select exactly the right clothes for every event above. Warm weather, rainy weather, cold weather, day, night and holidays. You will always look your best.

Advance Dating Workshop. 3 days, only eight guys go shopping with our expert all day Friday. Based on your age, height, weight, body type and skin tone, she chooses exactly the right attire for you: size, style, color and pattern. From alluring patterned ties to dark ox blood shoes and belts. She even helps you with attaché cases, pens and wallets!

Back in the classroom on Saturday, learn about patterns in ties, casual shirts, sweaters, and slacks, what colors in patterns go together so that you stop making fashion mistakes every woman knows! Details include understanding seasonal colors, dressing for extreme cold, heat and what to wear on a warm summer evening for an outdoor concert. She shows you how to put together your advanced attire to create outfits that catch every woman's eye for major holidays such as Valentine's Day and Christmas parties.

A major benefit is that our expert does role playing with everyone individually so that she can identify each individual's ability with social graces and dating skills.

Learn dining out etiquette including table manners, ordering for the lady, and her and the sophisticated method of paying the check and appropriate tipping for service that always impresses women.

She guides you thru handling yourself on the coffee date: greeting, getting drinks, conversation, revealing yourself, active listening, responding to her revelations, ending the get together. Then she role plays with you as you call after the coffee date to set up a second get together such as lunch or pizza and beer date.

During second get together, she shows you how to handle Inevitable Questions as well as how to reveal and respond, touch when socially appropriate, compliment, actively listen and on and on.

For the Romantic Date, she helps you with setting up the dinner date, picking her up, how to conduct yourself at her front porch and home, and what to talk about at dinner and then how to end the evening gracefully.

SBP, BOX 807, WHITTIER CA 90608

CASH, CHECK OR MO PAYABLE TO SBP

CREDIT CARDS AT www.rdonsteele.com

ALL 7 BOOKS ONLY $99

How To Date–Volume 1	$25
How To Date–Volume 2	$29
Threesome	$25
One-Hour Orgasm	$25
Sexpectations	$22
The Man's Guide To Women	$18
Dating 101: Instant Cure for Romanc Blues	$22

ALL 5 VIDEOS ONLY $159

2-vcd The Right Attitude Workshop	$59
2vcd Body Language-Steel Balls Principles	$49
3-vcd Body Language-Success with Women	$49
2-vcd Steele on Television	$49
2-vcd Don and A&E Love Chronicles	$49

ALL 3 RADIO SHOWS ONLY $59

Volume 1 RADIO 30 HOUR MP3	$29
Volume 2 RADIO 30 HOUR MP3	$29
Volume 3 RADIO 30 HOUR MP3	$29
Reinforce Set—best of 200 interviews 2 audio cds	$29
Playgirl Interview audio cd	$5
BBC Interview audio cd	$5

EVERYTHING IS POSTAGE PAID
PRIORITY/ FIRST CLASS USA AIR MAIL INTERNATIONAL

FREE VIDEO
www.rdonsteele.com/rds_video.html, www.rdonsteele.com/don_bio.html

FREE AUDIO
www://steelballsradio.com, www.rdonsteele.com/free_audio.html

FREE NEWSLETTER
Send email with subject SUBSCRIBE to
mosbnewsletter-subscribe@yahoogroups.com